John C. Jac

Railway Tales

ANJR Publishing

Cover Picture: John C. Jacques hands the single line token to the driver
of Jubilee "Ulster" hauling a passenger railtour as it passes Measham box in 1963.

First Published in Great Britain in 2001 by ANJR Publishing

1 3 5 7 9 10 8 6 4 2

ISBN 0-9540731-0-X

Story illustrations by Donna Lapworth.

With thanks to Joy, Kelly, Mike, Sam
and all those who inspired, helped and contributed
to make this book possible.

WWW.RailwayTales.co.uk

John C. Jacques

Railway Tales

John C. Jacques

JOHN C. Jacques was born in Shackerstone, Leicestershire in 1925 and has spent most of his working life in the local area. In 1940 he joined the London Midland & Scottish Railway (L.M.S) as a junior porter, 'The Station Lad'. His jobs would include trimming and maintaining the signal lamps, the loading of livestock and collecting sack bills from the farms, apparently not a job for the faint hearted. John also blames the length of his arms on the amount of lamps he had to carry to distant signals!

In 1943 John was called up and served in the Army for five years. He fought through France, Belgium, Holland and Germany.

When he returned home he decided to follow in his Fathers footsteps and trained as a Signalman. His first postings were along the old Ashby and Nuneaton Joint branch line before its closure. He then moved onto Bagworth signalbox, Coalville Town Crossing and finally Bardon Hill Crossing. Like most signalmen he had a pastime to while away the minutes between trains. John's hobby was writing short stories.

In 1990 he retired from the railway after 50 years service, but this was not to be the end of his association with his working life. He is now the curator of the Museum on the preserved Battlefield Line at Shackerstone in Leicestershire.

Foreword

IN 1940 I was a Junior Signal Lamp Lad on the London Midland & Scottish Railway, bringing the lamps to the lamp cabin, filling them with paraffin, trimming the wicks, lighting them and taking them back up the signals.

I would try to get lifts to the far away distant signals on motor trolleys, brake vans, engines, freight trains — anything to save walking, anxiously clutching my lamps to save them from getting knocked over.

On cold or wet days, sanctity would be sought in signalboxes, platelayers' cabins, shunters' cabins or the porter's room. Gradually the heat from the fire would start my paraffin-soaked trousers to steam and the smell would get me banished to the cold world outside once again.

The tales in this book are about the life of railwaymen fifty years ago, an era that will never return. They open a time capsule releasing yesterday's nostalgic memories to capture the imagination for a brief while. With the future uncertain, the present traumatic, we turn more and more to the comfort of the past.

I hope these gentle, humourous stories will do just that.

John C. Jacques.

60 years on, the station "Lad" arrives at Shackerstone
on the same bicycle he used on his first day.

To my wife, who encouraged me to write and always enjoyed my stories.

*My thanks to Mrs. Burns Morton who kindly
typed the manuscript from my scribbles.*

When time, who steals our years away,
Shall steal our pleasures too,
The memory of the past shall stay,
And half our joys renew.

Thomas Moore

TREACLE & FRED

THE platelayers arrived at their cabin to start the day — two on foot and one on an ancient bicycle with an oil lamp on the front. He only rode it to work; going home there was no room for him on the machine at all; it was taken up by old fence rails, gate posts, tree branches, split sleepers, anything combustible to keep his hearth and home warm without payment. He never failed to find what he called, "Me bitt er wood", he was known as "Owd Woody".

"Jober" and the Ganger walked together, holding their "pigeon baskets". These were wicker baskets with a hinged lid fastened with a long wooden peg through two hoops, containing the men's lunch wrapped in newspaper and a small, thick green glass bottle with the words "Lung Tonic" moulded on to the side, filled with milk.

They all went through the morning ritual saying, "Ay-up" to all, being, "Ay-upped" in return.

The platelayers' cabin was built with

old sleepers stood on end and let into the ground for the walls. The roof was made of large slates. The gaps and bolt holes in the sleepers were stuffed with rags and tarred tarpaulin strings, rather like caulking a ship's timbers. The brick floor was shattered to pieces, after years of stick-chopping on rainy days.

The door had a large hole at waist level covered from the inside with the cracked glass door from an old clock. It served as a peep-hole so that the platelayers could look out down the path for unwelcome official visitors.

Inside, an open brick fireplace and chimney lined one wall, the original fire bars long burnt away and replaced with fishplates. A double row of sleepers, propped up on bricks, lay along each wall providing the seating arrangements. Old seed sacks, scrounged from farm buildings, were folded and put on the rough seats to give only small comfort to the corduroy-trousered bottoms. A wide length of wood, nailed to the whitewashed wall above the seats, was polished by years of restless backs rubbing along it.

Each man had his own position on the sleeper seat and kept to it, like a cow that always goes to the same stall in the milking shed.

Above, on two beams, lay four scythes with rusting blades, long wooden rails, posts, jack handles, stiff bristled brushes and spare bundles of bean sticks. On the walls hung axes, slashers, billhooks, augers, a crosscut saw, an adze, dollys, boltbreakers and spanners. They looked like weapons in a mediaeval castle. At one end were shovels, picks, crowbars, barbed wire, riddles, jacks, a stock of new wooden rail keys and a two-man drilling machine. Still at the same end were also an oil can and two buckets, a bundle of rolled-up green, red and yellow flags, plus a large bag of salt. On the sill of a very small window lay four mildewed rule books, engraved with the words "For Company's Servants Only" on the sun-faded cover. They were never opened and only the spiders seemed to be interested, determined to bind them shut forever.

A pile of sticks, made from old sleepers chopped the previous day, lay under the seat ready to light the fire that soon blazed away under a four-pint cast-iron kettle resting on two fishplates over the flames. The platelayers left their wicker baskets in the cabin (cloth bags were never used; the mice would be gnawing at the food as soon as their backs were turned) and went off to scrape and oil the points in the shunting yard, knowing quite well the kettle wouldn't be boiling for some time.

The fourth member of the gang, "The Walking Man", lived at the other end of the length. He started there every morning to walk the Permanent Way, clutching his badge of office; a special long-handled hammer with which he knocked back into place all the wooden keys that had fallen out from the rails during the night.

He was a bachelor and lived in a railway cottage with his best friend, Fred, a nondescript dog with the legs of a greyhound and the body of a rough-haired terrier. He was a happy man, not too good with the printed word, but expert on all the wildlife along the railway bank and in the woods. His loves were food, beer, tobacco and Fred. His stomach was enormous and hung like an avalanche ready to fall. His trousers were held together tightly by a broad leather band from some discarded horse harness. All the local people knew him as "Treacle Belly", and he was quite proud of the name.

The railway ran right through the centre of a large sporting estate owned by Sir Joshua Crabtree-Bough, who had allowed the railway to be built because he was short of cash at the time and they also offered him free first-class travel.

The railway banks and woods were full of wildlife, including partridge, pheasant and rabbits. Fred and Treacle did their best to keep the numbers down with snare, ferret and catapult. Treacle couldn't "abide them noisy guns" and looked down on people striding over fields shooting for killing's sake. He was a deadly shot with his "Catypult" made with thick, square elastic purchased from the local Ironmonger.

All the villagers worked on the Estate and lived in tied cottages. They did not dare to poach game for fear of losing their jobs and homes.

Treacle was a king amongst them. He could stroll through the Estate on the railway, a big canvas bag on his shoulder containing a few wooden keys. It was like a diplomatic bag and could transport fur and feather away in legitimate pursuit of his work, much to the disgust of the Gamekeeper.

Treacle had a good barter system going. What game he and Fred couldn't eat he exchanged for beer, tobacco, sausages, home-cured bacon, pork pies and secondhand clothes. He did not rate money very highly, which was just as well because the villagers didn't have any to spare anyway.

A week before Christmas, Treacle always got official orders to go "rabbitting". That meant getting at least twenty-five rabbits from the railway banks to send to the Permanent Way Head Office Staff, who in turn gave them to friends and relatives in town as Christmas presents, without costing them a penny.

Treacle always sent his own Permanent Way Inspector, Mr. Percival Smallwood, known as "Owd Sawdust" a large cardboard box with his name on it, securely tied with binder twine. Inside, wrapped in paper and straw, lay two large rabbits with their fur jackets removed, cleaned and ready for the pot, nestling alongside two plump pheasants with their feather coats off, drawn and ready for the pot. A similar box went to the Stationmaster, Mr. Samuel Barker, known as "Owd Doggy".

The poached birds were never mentioned and a discreet silence was kept between all parties. In fact, "Doggy Barker" never spoke to Treacle at all! But letters of complaint from Sir Joshua Crabtree-Bough, concerning diminishing game in the woods alongside the railway were quite often accidentally dropped into the fire.

A demand from "Owd Crabby" that, "All game killed by moving trains should be returned to the Estate Office", brought smiles to the staff of the Permanent Way.

Treacle used to lay a trail of corn and raisins down the bank in chosen positions where he could lie in waiting, then "Zonk" them with a well-placed stone from his catapult, all in near silence and without having to set foot in Owd Crabby's estate.

Treacle and Fred arrived at the cabin just as the tea was being brewed, using a black half-gallon chipped teapot that had started out in life in some unknown railway refreshment room. Four large, battered pot mugs, with the Company's initials embossed down the side and from the same unnamed source, stood waiting. They opened their baskets. Breakfast had begun.

Opening a wooden box. Treacle took out a large frying pan and, with a knife, scraped out a generous portion of dripping into it from a tin marked Bourneville Cocoa. Next, he took out four sausages, two thick slices of fat, home-cured bacon and two eggs. He soon had them sizzling on the fire. Two thick slices of bread washed down with a pint of black tea would keep him going until lunchtime.

Fred, lying on his bag under the seat, was tired after a long walk; the last mile he spent on top of the rail itself. The rough ballast made his feet sore, but he soon found a smoother path on top of the rail.

His master, having eaten his own breakfast, started to get Fred's from a tin in his bag. He took four partridge eggs, acquired on the morning walk, broke them into the pan, and with some leftover crusts, gave Fred his first meal of the day. The frying pan was licked clean, then put away in the box all ready for next time.

Treacle put his hand into his diplomatic bag and groped around. "I've gotter nat", he said, bringing out a curly brimmed bowler hat with bits of rabbit fur sticking to it. They each solemnly

tried it on in turn, but it was too small.

"Appen it's Owd Crabtree's", said Jober.

"Nar, ee woodna get is gret yed in it", replied Treacle, and he would know having found two of Sir Joshua Crabtree-Bough's hats in the past. The first he handed into the Station Clerk and waited expectantly for the customary silver threepenny piece reward, sixpence if you were lucky. But no, nothing. He knew Owd Crabby had claimed it; news had filtered through the grapevine. Treacle never returned any of the honourable knight's headgear again.

Whilst travelling on the local trains, Sir Joshua Crabtree-Bough and the tenant farmers had a habit of standing by an open window, gazing out over the Estate, looking at the state of the crops, game, sheep, cattle and workers who had stopped to light a pipe or were sitting under a tree. They had a grandstand view going up the embankment, but it cost them dearly in the loss of headgear.

Sir Joshua, leaning out to get a better view of a plough team that had stopped for some reason, lost an almost new deerstalker. When he got back to the station, he demanded that it should be searched for immediately, but it had still not turned up twenty-four hours later. It was brought up during conversation in the platelayers' cabin.

"Owd Crabby lost another 'at", said Jober.

Treacle made no comment; he knew quite well where it was — hanging on a nail behind his pantry door. He was going to wear it himself on cold nights. The rear peak had been cut off with his razor-sharp shutknife because he thought it looked daft.

Sir Joshua became quite persistent about his hat. Everytime he met the Stationmaster he insisted that it should be, "Searched for with greater diligence." Stationmaster Barker passed the message to the Clerk, who passed it to the Senior Porter, who passed it to Jimmy, the Junior Porter, known as "the Lad". Two days later he went to the door of the platelayers' cabin.

They were playing dominoes during an extended lunchtime. It looked like rain so they were, "'Anging on a bit." A large board rested across their knees from one seat to the other, its surface shining and glazed like a mirror from the action of the ivory dominoes. They "clicked" and "clacked" at every touch.

The men studied the dominoes in silence with as much concentration as an international chess match. The winning domino was crashed down on to the board by the jubilant player. Then the inquest began:

"Yo shudda pleyed yer thray."

"Ar cuddna pley it, ar 'ad to get me sevens out."

"Ar cuddna do nowt, ar 'ad four doubles."

"Yo blocked ma!"

"Ar diddna."

"Yo did!"

"Oose drop is it?"

They argued as though the stake was a sovereign rather than a penny, as it was moved up and down the board.

The Lad waited by the door. He knew better than to speak during the play.

"Ay up, Jimmy", they both said in unison.

"Ay up", he said in return. "Owd Doggy's sent a message. You've gotter search for Owd Crabby's 'at with er...", he paused; lines appeared on his forehead. He looked up at the rafters of the cabin as if for inspiration, "with a great GILLYDENCE!" They looked at him in silence, then Jober said, "A?" Treacle said, "Wot?"

Owd Woody scratched his head.

The Ganger said, "Gillydence?"

"Ar", said the Lad.

"Perhaps they're sending a dog wot snifs out 'ats", said Treacle, smiling.

Then a chuckle developed into a bellowing laugh that made his great belly wobble about like hot volcanic lava. Even Fred opened an eye and looked at his master, fearing he was going to have a seizure. They were all laughing now, so loud that it even got the Signalman off the locker and into the window. The joke soon got round about the "'at sniffing dog." The deerstalker was never found, and only Treacle knew the reason why.

The Permanent Way Inspector, Percival Smallwood, known as "Owd Sawdust", walked the length once a month, his progress going before him via the signalbox telephone, the Signalman making a special effort to get the message to the platelayers, "Owd Sawdust's about."

One cold day a young relief Permanent Way Inspector standing in for Percival Smallwood (he was off with a bad chest) approached the platelayers' cabin at lunchtime. That was a mistake for a start.

"Ay up", said Treacle, looking through the clock door spy hole, "somebody's coming."

The Ganger hastily pulled out his large Waltham pocket watch. "Owd on", he said, "tek no notis, wa've got ten minits yet."

They had knocked off for an early lunch an hour before, with the door tightly shut and a great roaring fire blazing in the cabin.

The Inspector pulled the door open and stepped inside. "I'm the relief Inspector", he said, "I've noticed a very poor..."

He took a breath, started to cough, then choked, his face went red, he clutched his throat, his eyes protruded and started to water, whistling noises were heard in his chest, his knees sagged. He managed to push himself out from the doorway into the open air and stood, gasping.

"Strewth", he said, "It smells a bit strong in there." The platelayers ignored him. "It's like something that's gone off dead. Can't you smell it?"

They all knew quite well what had "died". It was Treacle's feet. They smelled like a dead camel that had been left out in the Gobi Desert for a month, however, they were not going to tell that to a young upstart of an Inspector.

Treacle broke the silence, and with a solemn face said, "it must be the dreens."

"There aren't any drains", replied the Inspector sharply. "Is it that dog?"

"No, it ain't. My Fred 'ad a good wash in the rain the other day", said Treacle.

The Inspector sensed he was up against a united front and went on to list all the faults he had found on the Permanent Way and eventually left.

They watched him in silence as he walked off until he was out of sight.

"Your feet were a bit strong", the Ganger said.

"Ar, ah know", said Treacle, "but ah canna 'elp it. Me owd Dad's feet were the same, it's irriditery." He blamed everything on his late father, with a sort of cheerful helplessness. His feet, his great belly, drinking, eating, and poaching were all passed off with, "It's me owd Dad's fault, it's irriditery." Even the dog's name was inherited; all the family dogs were called Fred.

They all left the cabin, Treacle and Jober carrying an axe and slasher went to the grindstone under a lilac tree that some forgotten platelayer had stuck in many years before by the door. The wheel was fastened across two upright sleepers let in the ground. With hard usage it had worn to an oval shape and seemed to go up and down, rather than around. The square in the centre had worn round so that the spindle had to be packed with wooden wedges.

Treacle pressed the axe on to the wheel and Jober turned the handle. All went well for a while. With his pipe drawing well and lost in a world of his own, Jober was quite oblivious to the fact that the wheel was stationary and that the spindle was going round and round. He was brought back down to earth with shouts from Treacle of, "Owd yer! Owd yer! Knock them wedges in!"

It was a long job sharpening the hedgecutting tools, and always ended with the plaintive cry, "Way sh'll 'ave ter ask Owd Sawdust for a new stoone."

Treacle took the tools back to the cabin to prepare for the walk back along the track towards home and to see "if them meece have eaten Fred." His only criticism of his dog was that he tolerated mice. Fred would let them play all around him in the cabin with complete indifference. "He'd let them meece tek the food outer 'is mouth", said Treacle. Fred ignored the mice. After running himself silly after rabbits and pheasants, he felt it was beneath his dignity to chase after them as they skipped all around him as he lay on his bag.

Treacle opened the cabin door. Fred woke up, wagged his tail, stretched and they were soon off home: Treacle, with his "Diplomatic bag" over one shoulder, keying hammer on the other, Fred daintily walking on top of the rail, the mice left to play around the dying embers of the cabin fire.

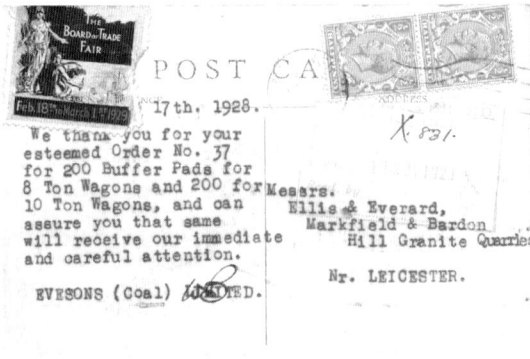

POST CARD

17th. 1928.

We thank you for your esteemed Order No. 37 for 200 Buffer Pads for 8 Ton Wagons and 200 for 10 Ton Wagons, and can assure you that same will receive our immediate and careful attention.

EVESONS (Coal) LIMITED.

X. 831.

Messrs.
Ellis & Everard,
Markfield & Bardon
Hill Granite Quarries

Nr. LEICESTER.

The Platelayer's Motor Trolley

IT was a fine summer morning, so the platelayers decided to go through to the far end of their three-mile section and lift a few sagging joints.

The doors of an old sleeper-built shed were opened and the morning sun shone on something looking like a canopied bed on wheels. It was a "Wickham" motor trolley with a wooden top and canvas side curtains, $3^1/_2$ horsepower, two cylinders and built around 1930. They trundled it out along a sleepered path, swung it round and dropped it on to the rails in the siding ready for running. A flat trailer was manhandled on to the rails behind and hooked up to the trolley. Tools were put on board; shovels, picks, jacks, a heap of small stone chippings, a riddle and a large spanner.

"Go and tell the Bobby[1] we're going with the trolley", said the Ganger. One of the men went off to the signalbox and came back with the message, "We can go now, so don't be long starting."

From the cabin, they got their lunch baskets, a ten-pint cast iron kettle full of water, a box of sticks and coal, and put them on the trolley. The Ganger inserted a long starting handle into the machine, then peered into its innards and made delicate adjustments. Everything was ready. He turned to one of the men, "Give 'er a turn, Albert."

Albert grasped the handle and turned for a number of minutes with only a slight hiss from the engine as a reward. Renewed effort achieved nothing. He stopped, overcome, and panted, "You 'ave a turn" to Billy Pottle, one of the other men standing around. The same thing happened. "'Er wunna go", cried Albert.

The Ganger made a decision, "Get the pencil", he cried. Not, "Have you got a pencil" or "Get a pencil", but, "Get the pencil." One of the men searched in a box, unwrapped a grimy piece of rag to reveal a plug spanner and a thick wagon-labelling pencil. The Ganger took the two plugs out and was handed the pencil. He took it like a surgeon taking a scalpel and proceeded to pencil all over the plug points. He did it from all angles, holding it this way then that. The other platelayers stood around watching intently as though he was Constable sketching his famous mill. They were never allowed to do this.

A strange voice broke the silence, "Wot's that do then, mate?" A fireman had crept up from a temporarily stilled shunting engine in the sidings, overcome with curiosity to observe the pencil ritual. They all turned and looked at him in silence for a minute, then one said, "It meks 'er goo."

The truth was that not one of them knew much about the engine at all; their only mechanical knowledge was limited to putting a chain on a push-bike, or mending a puncture, but they all had faith in the ritual of the pencil on the plugs.

The Ganger blew on the plugs gently, had one last look, then screwed them back in the engine. "You give 'er a turn now, Jober", he said to the other Platelayer.

Jober was a large, kindly fellow, always willing to please, ever ready to give away produce grown on a double allotment that backed up to the wall of the local tavern. Most Saturdays would find him working on his allotment. He always had his wheelbarrow with him. He was never without it. As soon as the tavern door opened, Jober was in demanding, "A pint o' the best." It was strong ale brewed on the premises, known as "Rot [Rat] Killer". The rats fell into the beer vats and were drowned. It was said that this enhanced the body of the beer.

As the night wore on, Jober, sitting in his favourite seat beneath a faded sepia photograph of a bearded village cricket team dated 1878, would get red and retell the tale of the motor trolley running away without anyone at the controls. Eventually, when he was unsteady on his feet, the Publican would hint that, "Perhaps that 'a better be the last pint", and this always brought forth the plaintive cry, "I'm as Jober as a Sudge." He never said it unless he had drunk

too much; it was like a built-in alcohol barometer for all the world to hear rather than see. It was for this phrase that he was known as "Jober".

"Get 'is barrer", someone said. That touched a chord in Jober's mind. "I want me barrer", he would cry like a dying man calling for a priest. They knew that if his hands were put on to the handles of the wheelbarrow and pointed in the right direction, he would walk right to his gate, where his wife would meet him, put him on the sofa and leave him all night. He always said his "barrer" used to lead him home. Without it he was lost.

One night, as a cruel joke, they pointed Jober and his "barrer" in the opposite direction. He went down the road as usual and started to turn right, but the turn wasn't there and he crashed into the church wall. He lay in the road with his arms around the wheelbarrow crying, "Me barrer, me barrer!", as though his favourite horse had collapsed and died. After a while they relented, fetched him back and this time pointed him and his wheelbarrow in the right direction, thus ensuring a trouble-free journey to his very gate.

This then was the man that grasped the starting handle.

With his coat off and hands full of spit, Jober turned the handle round like a mangle. The Ganger did mysterious things deep inside the engine compartment. It chuffed once. "Kape 'er gooing", shouted the Ganger. Jober, conscious of an audience, for the Fireman was still watching the performance even though he was a man who doubted the pencil ritual, rose to even greater heights and turned round the handle faster than ever. His eyes stuck out, the veins in his neck were like ropes, he panted for breath and drops of sweat fell off his nose.

The engine fired, stopped, fired again and continued to fire unevenly, but at least it kept going. Jober collapsed on to the ground and appeared to be having some sort of a seizure, but eventually got his breath back and said, "Ar told yer 'er 'ud go." He was triumphant; the honour of the gang had been saved.

The watching Fireman turned away baffled, and went back to the engine to tell the driver about the pencil and the plugs.

The Signalman had been to the window many times. Thirty minutes had passed since he gave permission for the trolley to go. He had seen the performance with the trolley many times before and had not pulled the ground signal off from the sidings. The engine of the trolley resumed a more even beat and the Ganger waved right away. The Signalman reluctantly pulled the signal off. The platelayers, grinning broadly, climbed on to the trolley to sit sideways like riding on an elephant at the zoo.

The Signalman watched them slowly disappear out of sight, knowing they would be quite likely to reappear in a half hour, pushing the trolley back towards his signalbox with engine failure.

The platelayers' motor trolley was responsible for many delayed trains, grey hairs and blasphemy, but all went well today, and after forty minutes the section was cleared, proving that the magic pencil had worked once again.

[1] 'Bobby' was the old name used for a signalman. This was because they had been railway policemen in the early days of the railways.

A—GENERAL INSTRUCTIONS RESPECTING THE WORKING OF MOTOR TROLLEYS FOR USE OF ENGINEERING DEPARTMENT'S STAFF.

(6) *In the event of a motor trolley being stopped by accident, failure, obstruction, or other exceptional cause and cannot be removed at once from the rails, the ganger or person in charge must arrange for the obstruction to be immediately protected in accordance with Rules 217A and 218 in the Book of Rules and Regulations.*

(7) *When it is necessary for a motor trolley to remain stationary on the line for any purpose for more than 3 minutes, the ganger or person in charge must arrange for the motor trolley to be protected in accordance with the Rules and Regulations in force for the protection of a ballast train stopping on the line.*

Old Ben and the Lad

MOTOR CARS WERE LESS THAN DUST TO OLD BEN

JIMMY the Junior Porter, known as "the Lad" rode his bicycle down the station yard to the goods shed. He was first that morning as usual. He lent his cycle against the shed and went across the lines to the signalbox to get the station key, stopping only to say, "Good Morning", to the signalmen. He made his way to the goods office built on to the end of the shed, ran up four worn sandstone steps, unlocked the door and soon had a fire roaring away with the sticks and coal that he had left ready the night before. He unlocked the inner door and stepped into the large goods shed. It was full of cattle feed, pig meal, calf meal, turkey pellets, poultry meal and every sort of food to feed everything on a farm, stacked in rows, some two bags high. One end held a stock of cement, also a pile of sundry items waiting to be delivered by the station lorry. In the middle of the floor stood a 30-cwt crane, firmly anchored in the ground beneath.

In the high glazed roof a flock of sparrows sat twittering on the girders. They had a good life, all the food they wanted down below and a dry place to live in. The same applied to the rats. Jimmy didn't like the rats. He stamped his feet as he walked across the shed and they scuttled out of sight beneath the floor. The rats had gnawed holes in

19

all the bags close to the wall and had an endless supply of food. He went down the five worn wooden steps to open the door across the rails. It weighed about half a ton and ran on a rail top and bottom. It needed some effort to open it but with the help of a crowbar and some puffing and panting, the Lad managed to slide it open. He dealt with the opposite door in the same way.

By this time the Senior Porter known as "Old Ben" put in an appearance, slowly riding his cycle down the station yard. He was small and bow legged, with a perpetual grin and a rheumy eye, wearing a railway uniform and a wide brimmed trilby hat from a long past era, no colour remained and the brim sagged down, all stiffening gone.

"Old Ben" who was a bachelor, had a rented acre, a few beasts, fowl and some ramshackle sheds. He had wanted to be a farmer but never made it. He was in the First World War driving horses and a limber. He used to tell young Jimmy some hair-raising tales about driving his horses through shot and shell. The Lad listened enthralled, believing every word.

"Morning, Ben."

"Morning, Jimmy. I nearly run over that rabbit at Paggetts Corner", said Ben. "I shall 'ave 'im one day." It was a standing joke about the rabbit. They all knew "Old Ben" couldn't run a tortoise over, let alone a rabbit, if he went any slower, he would fall off.

The Lad went off to light the fire in the Stationmaster's Office. Old Ben took the teapot over to the box to mash. Later on the station lorry arrived to take the bags of cattle food out to the farms. Ben loaded the lorry while the Lad went out with some of the signal lamps, that were trimmed and lit by the signalman.

Mid-morning saw the arrival of the goods trip train, it stopped at every station down the line bringing incoming traffic and taking loads out. There were three vans of cattle feed and four empty wagons, the vans were put in the end shed and set for unloading the wagons down the yard, so with a bit of smart work by the Lad with the shunting pole (Old Ben never used it) the train was soon away. Then, more lorries to load until lunch time.

The cast-iron kettle on the fire was boiling away ready for the tea, the Goods Clerk was busy writing, perched on a high stool, he kept slightly aloof from the porters except for "Good Morning", or "Would you get some coal?" or "Would you get some water", with his clerical grey suit and a celluloid collar and tea in a flask. He had his own portable wash basin. It looked like a cupboard, the top opened on a hinge to expose a pot basin with a plug at the bottom, you filled it from a jug at the side, when you pulled the plug it emptied into a bucket in another cupboard underneath. The Lad filled the jug and emptied the bucket as required, there was no piped water on the premises, all water was hand-pumped from a well at the station 200 yards away.

After lunch the Lad went to finish the lamps, Old Ben made a bee-line for the four empty wagons that came in on the trip train. He knew from experience they would yield all sorts of odd things. He was looking for nuts and bolts, bits of wood, metal plates, pieces of rope, wire, bits of tarpaulin sheet, anything to keep Ben's ramshackle sheds from falling down, he never went home at night without something in his bag or tied to his cycle. His greatest find was a wagon coming in as empty with the bottom covered a foot deep in assorted nails, it mattered not to Old Ben that they were reject nails with all the points flattened — he filled his lunch bag (a big one for the job) every day for weeks with the cycle tyres dangerously near the rims on the way home. He was always looking for long lengths of timber, if he found one, it would be strapped on to his cycle, not along the crossbar, but straight across the carrier, he would cycle home completely oblivious of six feet of timber sticking out across the narrow country roads. Motor cars were less than dust to Old Ben.

Jimmy the Lad sat on the bags looking up at the sparrows when Old Ben came out of the office looking like a St. Bernard that had lost its barrel. "The cement invoice has come", he said. They both stood silent. They hated the cement vans but knew that stocks were down and would soon have to be replaced.

Sure enough, on the tripper the next day there they were, two 10-ton cement vans. After putting them in the shed, Ben and the Lad ignored them all the rest of the day.

Next morning they were still there, mute and foreboding. After lunch the Clerk said, "I think we'd better have the cement out."

"I like the bloody 'we'", muttered Ben under his breath.

They had special overall trousers and jackets for the cement, so they reluctantly put them on and went to the shed to open the van door. The sliding door opened an inch and then stuck.

Ben peered through the crack, "They've been loaded up against the sodding door", he said, "Get the bar, Lad."

Both struggled with the bar and freed the sliding door open. Five bags fell to the shed floor with a thump. Two of them had been torn right across from a protruding bolt on the door and they were enveloped in a choking cloud of cement dust.

The cement came in 1-cwt. hessian bags that let the dust out at the slightest movement. It was an inch deep on the floor of the van. They got the heavy sack barrows and started to wheel the sacks out of the van across the shed to the empty space allocated for cement.

After an hour Ben said, "Let's have a blow, lad." They were covered from head to foot in cement dust, their faces grey with it. Old Ben's eyes had watered and ploughed a furrow in the cement down his cheeks. His high crowned hat looked like a white stetson on the Lone Star Ranger. The dust hung like a pall of smoke in the shed. Even the sparrows had gone.

They walked over to the cart hole to get a bit of fresh air. The Lad took off his railway cap and banged it against the wall in a cloud of dust. Old Ben took his trilby off — not for him the harsh treatment of wall-banging. He brushed it tenderly with his fingers. "That cement's spoiling my hat", he said in all seriousness. His face was a startling white in contrast with his ruddy dome — hairless as an egg. On the top was a knob like a walnut. When the Lad had first seen it, he had asked in all innocence, "What's that knob on your head, Ben?"

Ben grinned and immediately launched into a gripping tale of the First World War when a shell blast and overturned his limber, knocked him out and ending with the words, " and this 'ere knob never went down."

The Lad believed every word.

They struggled on until knocking off time then Ben brushed the van floor clear of spillage, half-filled his spare bag and strapped it on to his cycle carrier.

"That's better than a poke in the eye with a sharp stick", he said, a favourite saying of his when loading his cycle.

The weighbridge at the station stood at the top of the drive, by the entrance. It was built in the days when the longest vehicle was a four-wheeled horse-drawn dray which would stand with all wheels on the weighing platform. When lorries came along the wheels were far too far apart to go on the platform so they had to be weighed twice. The front half and then the rear half, added together and the unladen weight subtracted.

Inside the weighbridge was a long balance beam with a brass slide on it to indicate hundredweights and quarters. At the end hung small weights for the tons.

The whitewashed walls bore the marks of hundreds of pencilled calculations — additions and subtractions — and many a heated exchange was held with the driver before 2d was handed over for the ticket signed by the porter.

Old Ben wasn't very keen on adding and subtracting. So when a lorry approached the weighbridge there were always great shouts of, "Where's the Lad?", who when available did all the weighing.

At the month end came the dreaded

bill collecting time. The Lad didn't like this job but was always called upon to go. Old Ben said he was too old to bike all that way and why the hell couldn't they be sent by post. Some were, of course, but a lot within five miles were sent with the Lad. It saved the stamps.

He was allowed to use the station cycle — a big heavy machine with a plate on it saying "L.M.S." and the station name. Most bills were for farmers for L.M.S. sacks and goods sent by rail etc. Many farms lay at the end of long rutted muddy lanes and often the Lad would end up carrying the cycle, first arming himself with a stout stick cut from the hedge. He knew as he walked through the farmyard what it would be

like. Two large dogs barking and growling, looking like they would tear him to pieces appeared, and making enough noise to waken the dead. He held the cycle in front of him like a shield and managed to get to the side door. A woman appeared and looked at him in amazement, not speaking, but eventually the conversation began.

"Morning,er... I've brought the bills."

"What bills?"

"The bills from the station."

"The station?" Despite the fact he was in full railway uniform complete with L.M.S. on lapels and peaked cap.

"The Railway Station."

Conversation ceased.

The woman made no attempt to stop

the dogs barking — they crept closer and looked as though they hadn't had a square meal for weeks. The Lad clutched his bike and stick and wondered why they didn't go and tear a few fowl to pieces that were pecking in a nearby muckheap.

Then the conversation continued.

"I don't know anything about that." She hadn't taken the envelope from him yet.

He read the name and the farm to her. "Er...This is the farm?"

"Yes."

"It's a bill for some things you had from the station. I'm here to collect the money."

She reluctantly took the envelope, holding it as though it were going to explode.

"He sees to all that."

"Where is he?"

"He's ploughing in the twenty acre."

Silence fell. The dogs had got fed up with barking and just stood — looking. He knew from bitter experience that if he walked across the fields to find "he", he wouldn't have the money on him and wouldn't leave ploughing to walk to the house to pay, so he said, "I'll call again another day." The woman said nothing and watched him walk across the yard carry his cycle down the lane. That was his first call. He knew there would be many more like that.

When he arrived back at the station that evening, Ben was loading his cycle.

"Had a good day, lad?" he asked.

"No, I haven't. I'm covered in mud and nearly been torn to pieces by bloody wild dogs", he said.

Ben grinned and continued to strap two long pieces of timber crosswise on the carrier, sticking out at great risk to passing motorists. He also had a bag of something that clanged mysteriously. When Ben cycled slowly up the yard on his way home, the signalman opened the window and shouted, "I see you're travelling out of gauge again tonight, Ben. I'll put you through on a 2-6-3." A 2-6-3 was the out of gauge bell signal for trains that required the adjoining line to be blocked.

Ben said, "Arr", and carried on his own sedate way.

London Midland and Scottish Railway Company.

24

The Birthday Party

THE deep railway cutting was like an oven from the heat of an August sun. The rails were hot to touch and shimmered in a heat haze. Black, tar-like preservative oozed out from the wooden sleepers.

On the railway banks the plants of the rose bay willow herb (Epilobium Angustifolium for the botanist folks) had taken over. They grew four feet high and stood in serried ranks from top to bottom. The red flowers were now replaced by seeds and were floating about like thistledown in the thermal currents of the cutting. The seeds attached themselves to everything; rails, brickwork, trains, people, dogs,

sheep, even low flying aircraft.

The platelayers had been riddling ballast. Not by choice, you understand, but only through the insistence of the Permanent Way Inspector, a certain Mr. Smallwood, known as "Owd Sawdust".

It was a bad patch of ballast in the cutting, mixed with soil and coal slack. They had to dig it all out from beneath the sleepers, shake it through fine mesh riddles, then pack the clean ballast back under the sleepers. It was a dusty, backaching job.

Early afternoon found the platelayers stretched out on the bank in the shade of a cattle walk overbridge. They were all fast asleep, including Fred the dog, who must have been chasing an elusive rabbit in his dream the way his legs were pedalling and muffled "Woofs", puffed out his hairy cheeks.

The Ganger awoke with a start and sat up. He had been dreaming in his sleep and saw Owd Sawdust approaching. He tried to get up, but couldn't and had a terrible struggle in his dream. He looked round wildly for the dreaded Inspector, then suddenly realised it was a dream and mopped his sweating brow with a large red spotted handkerchief.

The other three platelayers lay as if struck by an instant plague. The nearest one, a man with a large girth known as "Treacle Belly", lay on his back with his mouth open. With every inhaled breath, he sucked in groups of floating seeds from the willow herb plants growing all around him where he lay. Some disappeared down his throat, others stuck to a large, discoloured, leathery-looking object he laughingly called his tongue.

The Ganger peered closer, fascinated, and wondered if they would take root and grow. Would they shoot up through the mossy glades of Treacle's brain?

An approaching train awoke the platelayers and reluctantly, with much mopping of dust-blackened faces, spitting, coughing and groaning, they staggered to their feet, collected their picks, shovels, jack, wheelbarrow and riddle. They slowly made their way back to the cabin two hundred yards away, to feed the dying fire with splintered sleeperwood, which crackled and fizzed under the still warm kettle. Soon, pint mugs of steaming tea were passed around to ease their parched throats and wash away the rose bay seeds.

The Ganger felt around inside a large pocket in his jacket which was hanging on a nail behind the door and eventually brought out a small square tin marked:

ERASMUS WILLS' SALT

A delicious effervescent drink, cooling and refreshing, cures biliousness, sick headache, derangements of the stomach, liver, kidneys. Assists nature. Cleanses the stomach, clears the tongue, purifies the blood, relieves the bowels, frees the kidneys. Allays feverish heat and cures heartburn, indigestion, constipation etc.

He took off the lid and peered inside. It contained half-smoked Woodbine cigarettes of various lengths. He shook the tin to move them around and gave each piece of cigarette a minute inspection. Two were taken out, examined carefully at both ends, then rejected. The third one met his approval and was placed in his mouth.

He replaced the lid and put the tin back in his pocket, then selected a long splinter of sleeperwood and stuck the end in the fire. It flared brightly and was then applied to the end of the cigarette in his mouth.

He puffed away like a banking engine, then inhaled a large quantity of smoke and held his breath as if to trap it in his lungs forever. But after a few seconds his respiratory system started to reject it and forced it back out with a body-wracking cough, then another and another, turning his face a crimson hue.

The Ganger's eyes bulged ominously and seemed in danger of being shot out across the cabin. He clapped his hands up to them as if to press them more firmly back into his head.

He drew a deep breath and another stomach-wrenching cough started. His cap flew off, the heavy silver watch chain he wore across his waistcoat thrashed up and down, and it looked as though his watch would be snatched out of his pocket. Dust flew from his clothes with the convulsions of his body.

Three slates on the cabin roof slid fractionally downwards. Spiders that had ventured out to repair the perimeter of their web scuttled back in alarm to the innermost depths of sanctuary.

A group of woodworms in the rafters, forced to the surface of their holes by the extreme heat, were shaken off by the blast and dropped straight into Treacle's pint pot of steaming milkless tea. They were cooked in seconds and gulped down by the unsuspecting Treacle who declared it to be, "A grand drop 'a tay."

The Ganger's body spasms gradually subsided; he wiped his streaming eyes, puffed on his diminishing Woodbine, had a drink of tea and declared, "Cor, that's better."

The other occupants of the cabin took not the slightest notice of the Ganger's performance.

Treacle sat with his eyes closed, his dog Fred lay on a sack under the seat.

Woody just stared into the fire.

Billy "Me Legs Wunner Goo" Pottle sat reading a three-day-old newspaper with the aid of a thick bull's-eye glass he had found on an old signal lamp case (his eyes were weak as well as his legs). He had got the newspaper from the Signalman who had got it from the Porter, who had spotted it in an empty compartment on the evening train. This was the usual peculiar source of all their reading material. Billy was a long, thin individual with a slow ponderous gait and the largest, flattest feet you ever saw that stuck out at right angles. You had to stand well clear when he moved or you would get scythed down by his feet.

Woody (he never went home without "me bitter wood") broke the silence, "It's me birthday on Saturday", he said. Treacle awoke with a muttered oath and started to slap his thigh like a Bavarian folk dancer. He had fallen asleep with a cigarette in his mouth and it had fallen out on to his lap. He was always doing that trick. The food, the tea and the hot fire soon lulled him into dreamland.

The front of his corduroy waistcoat and trousers were pockmarked with small holes and scorch marks. He looked as though he had been challenged to a duel by a man with a red hot poker — and lost! When the cry, "Summat's burning!" went up, the first place to check was Treacle's clothing.

The Ganger spoke to Woody. "Your birthday, eh. What's 'er buying you then?"

"Nowt", was the reply.

"What's she usually buy you?"

"Nowt."

"What do you buy 'er?"

Woody frowned and tried to recall. "I once bought 'er a bottle of lavender water", he said slowly. "But 'er never used it."

Treacle, having put out the fire in his trousers, joined in the conversation:

"Why didn't 'er drink it then?", he asked.

"Drink wot?"

"The lavender water."

"Yerdunna drink it, yer puts it on yer."

Silence fell. Treacle, a bachelor, skilled in the ways of fur, feather, ferrets and dogs, pondered on the mysteries of women. "Put it on yer wot?" he enquired.

"It's to make yer smell nice", said the exasperated Woody, and stomped off out of the cabin to search for his bit of wood for his fire at home.

The other platelayer put the newspaper and bull's-eye glass down and said with a smile "It's a pity we 'aven't got a bucket full o' that lavender water, then Treacle could put 'is feet in it."

Treacle's feet were notoriously smelly. It was said that if he took off his boots and stuck his feet down a rabbit hole, the rabbits would come out with their paws up!

He took it all in good part and blamed it on his old Dad, whose feet used to smell the same. "I can't 'elp it, it's irry-ditt-arry", he said in all seriousness.

"We ought to have a party for old Woody", the Ganger said. "He doesn't get much from life."

It was true Woody's wife was very houseproud and wouldn't let him smoke or wear his boots in the house, so he spent most of his time in a shed in the garden. He had made the shed from old railway sleepers, fencing rails and bits of wagon tarpaulin. A glass cupboard door had made a window. With a brake van stove inside for cold evenings it was a snug haven where Woody could sit and smoke his pipe and keep on his boots.

The other two men agreed about the party, but money was short and it was the wrong time of year for selling pea and bean sticks. In the end they had to reluctantly fall back on the horseradish plan. Great clumps of horseradish plants grew in selected places on the railway banks and some years ago the Ganger's wife had made a few jars of horseradish sauce for the jumble sale. One had been purchased by the Vicar and had brought many an ecclesiastical tear to the eyes of visiting clergy, after spreading it too liberally on their roast beef, but they frequently begged for a jar to take away.

The local tavern keeper at the Blacksmith's Arms also found a good use for the powerful condiment, it was spread on his cold beef sandwiches, eagerly sought after by learned historians after visiting the local Battlefield (where King Richard III was slain in 1485). They, too, requested jars of local root to give to unsuspecting friends.

The Ganger's wife refused to make any more. After putting it through the mincer her eyes were red for days, and the smell never left the house for a week.

When Billy Pottle acquired an old mincing machine (thrown out when his aunt Ada died) the Ganger suggested that they make the horseradish at their cabin and share the cash. This they did and had a ready market for their efforts ever since.

The Ganger lit a small half-smoked cigarette and had another coughing bout as they slowly walked back to their cabin at the Station and then home.

The next morning brought steady rain which turned into a torrential downpour. The platelayers sat in their cabin, quite content to gaze out at the rain, drinking large mugs of tea and wondering whether or not to get out the domino board.

Across the path stood a corrugated iron lamp cabin, with the door open. Leaning against the metal door frame was the Junior Porter, known as "the Lad", waiting for the rain to stop before going out with the newly trimmed signal lamps.

It was also the day the platelayers filled their bottles (specially kept for the job) with paraffin, known as "ile". The platelayers had many uses for it – in bike lamps, table lamps at home, putting a drop on a dead fire to boil a kettle (although this use often set the chimney on fire) soaking sticks in it for the same purpose and for starting bonfires. The only other source of paraffin was once a week from the travelling ironmonger. He had a four-wheeled cart with a roof on, piled high with household requirements, from tin baths, buckets, dolly pegs, possers, saucepans and barrel vinegar to soap , buttons, clothes pegs, lamp glasses and wicks. Underneath the cart was a blacksmith-made twenty-gallon tank with a brass tap containing paraffin. He was known as the "Ile Man".

He measured the paraffin with two ancient pewter jugs, one for a pint, the other a half pint. One day a learned historian visiting the local Battlefield (1485) saw the pewter jugs and offered to buy them, or to replace them with two proper measures officially stamped with pint and half-pint marks, "To make it easier to measure the paraffin", he said.

If he had expected any gratitude he was mistaken. The Ile Man was highly indignant. "Sell me owd jugs", he gasped, "Wot do I want to sell them for? They 'ad belonged to me owd Dad and owd Grandad, and they measured ile with 'em ad that's good enough for me!"

He didn't want any new-fangled measures with marks on either, so the learned historian went off rather crestfallen and wished he had never mentioned the jugs. The truth was the Ile Man knew quite well he could get nearly nine pints to a gallon using his old pewter jugs!

The rain still pelted down, the muddy water swirling past the cabin door. Billy spoke, "It's a good job it isn't snow or it would be over our 'eads and we wouldn't be able to get outer the cabin."

"We could tunnel out", said the Ganger.

"Ow would we know which way we were going?" enquired Billy.

"We should 'ave to keep going up to the surface like moles and 'ave a look", said the practical Ganger.

"We could tunnel up to the Blacksmith's for some ale, then call for some bread from owd Crusty Spice [the baker] and come back to the cabin."

"We wouldn't 'ave to goo 'ome at all." Woody said with a beaming smile, delighted at the thought.

They all fell silent, each one busy with his own thoughts.

"A loaf of bread beneath the bough, a flask of wine and thou", murmured the Ganger.

"A?" said one

"Wot?" said another

"Omar Khayam."

"Wos ee lost in the snow?"

"Naw, ee was in the desert."

"Oh."

A book of poems had been found in an empty first-class compartment by the Station Staff. They had soon lost interest and had given it to the Signalmen, but it didn't last long there and the next stop was the platelayers' cabin where the Ganger read it and started to quote from suitable poems.

"Couldn't we call for a bit of cheese to go wi' the bread?" This request came from Treacle.

"You're allus thinkin' about yer belly", said Billy.

The rain stopped and the spell was broken, so the platelayers reluctantly got ready to go out to oil the points and

start their day.

They decided to get the horseradish on Saturday morning and needed the motor trolley for the job. The motor trolley was pushed out of its wooden shed and swung on to the rails in the siding, then loaded with two tin baths, four buckets, picks and shovels.

A long starting handle was inserted into the machine from the front. After much winding, puffing and panting, cursing, plug cleaning and fiddling with small screws in the engine, it reluctantly fired and eventually settled down to an uneven beat.

The Ganger instructed Woody, "Goo and tell the Bobby [Signalman] we're ready and only want to drop a few fence posts and wire off, then through the other end. We shan't be long."

Minutes later, the ground signal came off, starting signal came off, and the motor trolley chugged its way into a three-mile section.

About a mile onwards they stopped. On the side of the track grew in profusion the three-feet-high broad, green leaves of the horseradish plant. They were soon digging away to get at the thick, white roots growing deep down in the hard soil.

They dug in silence, gradually filling the tin baths, oblivious of passing time.

A light engine on the opposite line clanked to a halt. They looked up. The driver got down and walked over to them and spoke. "The Bobby wants to know what the hell you're doing. You've been gone an hour and are holding two trains up!"

The three platelayers stood in silence and looked at the Ganger. He was the boss, the spokesman at times like this.

The Ganger barely hesitated. "We 'aven't been 'ere all that long", he said. "I've only just looked at me watch."

He pulled out a battered watch on the end of a thick chain. "Look!" He stopped and peered closer at the watch, alarm showing on his face. "'Ere, wait a minute." He held it to his ear. "It's stopped." He shook it; it rattled. "Cor, summert's loose inside! And the 'ands are stuck. Me watch is broke", he cried in anguish. "It must 'a been when that starting 'andle swung round and 'it me this morning." It's me owd Uncle Joe's watch. I dunno wot 'ee'd say!" It was a heart-rending performance by the Ganger.

His companions said nothing and stood with solemn faces. They had seen the watch routine many times before. The Ganger tried it on all new faces – drivers, signalmen, inspectors, to explain loss of time, and often it got them out of trouble. They knew what his Uncle Joe would say – nothing, because he was dead.

Joe was trying to poke starlings' nests out of the louvres in the Church bell tower (because the Vicar offered him money) when he fell off the ladder and killed himself. Mind you, it should be pointed out that he was aged seventy-five at the time. He was wearing that watch when he fell; that's why something rattled inside and it had stopped.

The driver turned away without another word, climbed back onto his engine, jerked the regulator and chuffed off.

The platelayers loaded the full baths of horseradish root on to the trolley, got aboard and trundled off to the other end of their section. They were all grinning as if amused by something.

By lunchtime they were back at their home station cabin and after the Stationmaster and Clerk had gone home they started "Operation Horseradish".

The white roots were scrubbed clean in water from the rain barrel, cut into small pieces and fed into the mincing machine which was screwed to a post outside. They had tried doing it inside, but the fumes from the minced root were so strong that it drove them outside.

Each man had a turn on the handle of the mincer. Even so, streaming eyes were the order of the day, but they were certainly not bothered by flies; they would have dropped dead at five paces.

Eventually, a tin of ground horseradish was ready to be mixed with a quart of vinegar purchased from the Ile Man and well stirred with a flat piece of wood.

It was now ready to be put in the jars. Screw-top jars were hard to come by and all empty ones had to be returned to the platelayers. Some had originally contained "Prune Jelly", "Malt and Cod Liver Oil Extract", "Honey" or "Virol". But all had screw-top lids ideal for containing the strong horseradish.

Soon, all the jars were filled and the lids screwed down tightly. It was a large order. The doctor, vicar, tavern keeper, numerous farmers and the housekeeper at the Big House all wanted some. It would be paid for on delivery, thus enabling the platelayers to look forward to a bit of a party on Saturday for Owd Woody's Birthday.

One morning, some weeks before, when they were all in the cabin having breakfast, Treacle announced, "I've got a grannyphone!"

Woody asked, "A?" Billy followed immediately, "Wot?"

The Ganger seemed surprised and enquired, "A gramophone! Where did you get that from?"

Treacle, having gained their rapt attention, launched into the tale of the gramophone.

It started its life at the Hall, purchased by Sir Joshua Crabtree-Bough for his three bored daughters so that they could entertain their friends in the music room. Soon the ladies were flashing their ankles and dancing to the very latest tunes of the day, under the fixed, disapproving gaze of a marble-sculptured bust of Beethoven standing on a plinth in the corner. After two years, the gramophone was replaced by a newer model, and the Butler acquired it.

Its next move was to the Head Gardener's house, where the family played it until the spring broke. Then it was relegated to one of the outbuildings. It was there that Treacle saw it. He was there at the request of the Head Gardener who was troubled by a plague of moles. Treacle not only made his own wooden mole traps, but knew where to set them in their runs to catch the little underground tunnellers.

He had been shown how to do this by an old mole catcher, Mr. Titus Field, known as "Moley Field", long since dead, but his skill lived on in Treacle.

After some discussion with the Head Gardener, a deal was struck. Treacle would trap the moles in exchange for the gramophone and a box of records. It was a large cabinet type and stood two foot six high on three slender bowed legs and a brick; one leg had broken off.

Not being one to dally, Treacle borrowed a large wheelbarrow and wheeled his prize away.

The next move was to call on "Clockie Deacon", a local man who built and repaired grandfather clocks, to see if he could repair the broken gramophone spring. It was examined and pronounced repairable, although the spring was made shorter and required extra winding. A plump, dressed pheasant changed hands and later that week, the gramophone was wheeled back to Treacle's cottage, from where scratchy sounds of music issued forth every night and all and sundry were invited to, "Come and listen to me grannyphone!"

It was generously offered for the birthday party and enthusiastically accepted. The Ganger said they would fetch it with the motor trolley on Saturday morning.

"Wot sort is it?", someone asked.

"An Alba", said Treacle.

They all looked blank. "A woter?" enquired Woody.

"An Alba", Treacle replied.

Silence fell; they had never heard of that name. "Is it the sort where that little terrier dog is looking down the 'orn listening to 'is 'owd dad's voice?"

That question from Billy "Me Legs Wunna Goo" Pottle brought a loud "Naw", from Treacle.

A discussion about what the dog was listening to started. One thought it wouldn't be possible to tell his dad's voice from a parrot being strangled on that scratchy old record.

"It's a bone they put down there", was another suggestion.

Silence fell once again. Then Woody had the answer. "It's meece [mice]", he said.

"A?" "Wot?" "Meece, where?" they chorused.

"Down the 'orn on the grannyphone!" shouted Woody. "They put some meece down the 'orn and the terrier dog can 'ear them a'scrabbling about!"

They digested this, and finally agreed that mice could quite well be the answer.

It was still being discussed as they walked slowly down the line, each one carrying a scythe over his shoulder to cut down the prolific rose bay willow herb that grew on the banks of the cutting. Billy was well to the rear of the group. "Me legs wunna goo this morning!" he said, and when he got to where they were scything, he had to have a sit down, "on account of me legs."

The day of the birthday party dawned and after they had oiled the points and had breakfast, they pushed the motor trolley out of the shed and onto the rails in the siding. They then went through the ritual of winding, anointing the plug electrodes with a thick lead pencil and winding again before the engine reluctantly fired and eventually carried them slowly and noisily forward and out on to the main line. A good run was made today, both ways, and they were back within the hour with the gramophone hidden under a piece of wagon sheet.

It was carried into the cabin, where they all stood around whilst Treacle proudly unveiled it.

He lifted the lid and propped it open. It exposed a brown velvet covered turntable; on either side was a lever, one to make it revolve faster or slower, and another for putting on the brake.

Two small metal recessed cups contained thick and thin steel needles for loud or soft music. Golden letters proudly proclaimed,"THE ALBA GRAMOPHONE". Double doors opened at the front to reveal where the sound came out, with space on either side to hold all the records.

They were all suitably impressed and Treacle wanted to play the records immediately, but the Ganger decided it was too early and to wait until afternoon after the Stationmaster and Clerk had gone home.

At lunchtime Treacle and Woody, each clutching a sack half-filled with straw, were dispatched to the Blacksmith's Arms to acquire six quart bottles of the Landlord's best beer known as "Rot [Rat] Killer", because the rats also liked a drink of the best beer and often fell into the open vats during the brewing process and drowned.

A call at the butcher's to pick up a box containing four large pork pies completed their task.

They carried the sacks carefully back to the cabin and put the bottles on a plank resting on two bricks, already holding two quarts of Granny Birkett's parsnip wine. All drink and victuals were paid for from the sale of the horseradish sauce.

Woody's own offering was a large stone bottle of rice wine he had brewed in his shed. It was easy to make and needed no boiling, but was very potent. He used to make his wine in the house and boil the ingredients in the copper until that fateful night on his birthday when the Chapel Preacher called, as he often did, to play the old harmonium that had belonged to his wife's father.

Woody was drinking matured elderflower wine and asked the Preacher if he would "sup a glass?" with him. The answer was, "Well, it is a very cold night and it is your birthday, and after all it is only made from God's own fruits of the Earth", so, "Yes", he would have a glass, please.

After a glass (a large one), he declared it to be, "A splendid beverage." After three more glasses, he thought it was, "Wondrously relaxing."

He was playing the harmonium and it was to be noticed that something seemed to be lacking in the co-ordination between his hands and feet.

Two more glasses later, his fingers were playing the notes, but his feet wouldn't pedal the bellows. If he stopped playing, he could pedal away merrily, but he just couldn't use hands and feet together.

After filling their glasses again. Woody solved the problem. He got down on to his knees and pedalled the bellows with his hands whilst the Preacher concentrated on the music. They worked perfectly together. Both red of face and damp of brow, bellowing out stirring hymns, "fighting the good fight, marching with the Christian soldiers, ploughing the fields and scattering", in complete unison.

Woody's wife, being a non-drinker, looked on with growing alarm not quite knowing what to do or say.

They stopped for breath, but by now the Preacher was so relaxed he had to lie down on the horse-hair sofa.

He still lay there hours later, and eventually Woody had to push him home on Pincher Martin's handcart. Luckily he was a bachelor.

Woody's wife blamed him and swore him to secrecy. She banned all winemaking in the house.

It was three o'clock and they were all in the cabin sampling the pork pie and beer, with Treacle proudly selecting records and winding his beloved gramophone.

They thought, "Nowt" to a lady soprano and decided, "'er corsets were too tight." A strangulated tenor was dismissed with the words, "'ee sounds as if 'ee's wearing an ill-fitting appliance", or words to that effect.

The shortened spring suddenly slowing the record made the singer appear to be overcome by some mysterious torpor, only to be brought back to normality by rapid winding of the handle.

They played these records:

Norman Long, "A Song, A Smile and A Piano." Flotsam and Jetsam. Clapham and Dwyer. Layton and Johnstone. Jack Payne, "The Flies Crawl Up the Window Pane", "The Whistler and his Dog" – the barking dog at the end of this record brought Treacle's dog, "Fred", out from under the seat to investigate.

The afternoon Signalman came over to see what they were doing and was offered a drink if he had a cup. He was back like a shot with the largest mug he could find, which was generously filled with "Rat Killer" beer. He wasn't able to stay because he couldn't hear the box bells for the sound of the gramophone.

Billy's favourite tune was called "Charleston Charley", by the Carlton Hotel Dance Orchestra. It actually started his foot tapping and as time wore on and the level of the drinks went down, he stood up, lifted his feet off the ground and shook them about in time to the music.

The others looked on in amusement at Billy, who had difficulty at stepping over a rail, now danced about as if in a hypnotic trance.

His great feet, like flat planks of wood, flailed the air and stamped in time to the music. Dust rose from the floor, the coal bucket, dust pan and brush went flying, a pile of neatly stacked wooden rail keys were scattered and the bottles danced on the makeshift shelf.

"Eh up", "Eh up", "Owd it Billy! Owd it!" they shouted in alarm. "Watch them gret fate will yer! Yer'll ave the bottles o'er!"

They hastily gathered up the bottles and took them outside.

Billy was in full spate now; his cap had fallen off and was being pounded into the floor of the cabin. A combination of beer and wine had brought life back into his legs.

The shortened spring in the gramophone mechanism began to loose its power, the tempo slackened and lost its drive.

"Er's stoppin! Er's stoppin!" cried the dancing Billy, "Wind 'er up! Wind 'er up!"

It was Treacle who braved the flying feet and vigorously applied himself to the winding handle, bringing the music back to its original tempo.

The record eventually finished, the needle was lifted off and the brake applied to the turntable.

Billy collapsed, puffing and panting, onto the floor. He never danced again. That was his swan song, so to speak. He managed to drink another large mug of parsnip wine in the sitting position, then went to sleep with his head resting on a roll of barbed wire, and never felt a thing.

The Ganger took him home in the wheelbarrow. Being tall, Billy's head overhung at the front and the wheel rubbed an angry red mark on his bald head. He didn't feel that either.

Woody was helped on to his bicycle with The Ganger holding him one side and Treacle the other. They pushed him home and put him in his shed. He declared it was the best birthday party he had ever had.

Treacle fetched some empty grain sacks from the goods shed to make a bed. He was going to stay the night in the cabin. The Ganger walked home, leaving behind another episode that they would talk about with great pleasure and much laughter for months, or even years to come.

The Lampman

THE Lampman walked along the track towards his cabin. It was a fine, cold morning with little wind. He hated the wind; it had a nasty habit of blowing out his lamps just as he got to the top of a high signal post. He unlocked the door of the corrugated iron cabin, went in and started to light the lamps. Two shelves ran down one side, full of trimmed lamps. A good lampman never left empty lamps in the cabin. At the far end below a window, a bench with a metal top was littered with cotton waste and old lamp wicks. On the other side of the cabin, a forty-gallon drum of paraffin stood on a wooden trestle. The smell of the "Longlight"

paraffin was very overpowering. The shelves and the brick floor had been soaked in it for years, but the Lampman never smelled it; he had been on the job six days a week, also, for years.

He adjusted the flame on six big square lamps, the large "bull's eyes" making the flames look two inches across, clipping the handles together with a sawn link from a signal pulley chain. He strode off, three lamps in each hand, to the sixteen-signal gantry that stood over the four main lines. Leaving three lamps on the ground, he climbed up the near vertical ladder and on to the platform, then up the short ladders to the signal lamps, opening the lamp cases and exchanging the trimmed lamp for the one that had been burning for seven days and nights. As he changed the highest "fast" line lamp, the signal clanked to the "off" position. He always had to beware of this as the Signalman had no time to look to see where the Lampman was before he pulled over the lever.

Climbing down to the platform he waited, leaning on the handrail for the train, soon to appear in the distance, smoke streaming from the squat chimney and travelling at about 80 m.p.h. He never tired of watching the fast trains from the high vantage point, roaring directly beneath him. For a few seconds he was enveloped in a cloud of white smoke, cutting him off from the world below. However, it soon cleared and he carried on changing the lamps, then back to the cabin, trimming more lamps and out again until lunchtime.

You would always know a regular Lampman, his trousers from below the knees caught the paraffin that dripped from the lamps he carried. His boots would never shine, for they were soaked

in it too. When he wanted to have a warm and eat his lunch it presented a problem for the Signalman did not want him up in the box. If he went to the Station to the Porters' Room and stood by the hot stove, his trousers would start gently steaming, filling the place with hot "Longlight" paraffin vapour, bringing nasty remarks from the pressed-trousered, shiny-buttoned porters.

The Lampman decided to have his lunch with "Little Alfie". Little Alfie was a brake van cleaner who worked down the shunting yard where the brake van stood on the stop blocks, lighting the stoves, cleaning out and trimming the brake lamps. He hopped from one van to another with his brush, dustpan and can of paraffin, living in a world of his own. Alfie wouldn't mind him smelling of paraffin because he smelled of it too. So the Lampman had his lunch in a warm brake, a chat and a rest before venturing out into the everlasting round of keeping the signal lamps shining, and without which no trains could ever have run at night.

Sale Day

THE country railway station was quite an important one with a good passenger service, a busy goods shed and a weekly sheep and cattle sale. The man at the helm was Stationmaster Benjamin Harris, known as "Snuffy" because of the large amount of snuff he used to push up his nostrils. He was a large man with a bushy moustache that was joined at each end to muttonchop whiskers. A large gold chain fell in graceful curves from a buttonhole in his railway waistcoat to pockets on either side of his generous stomach. Two medallions clinked together on the chain depicting the athletic prowess of a much younger, thinner Benjamin Harris.

Benjamin's one indulgence was snuff. It turned his moustache brown, fell down his waistcoat, and even stuck to the caps of his highly polished shoes on damp days. A lot of it got into his waistcoat pockets too. Every time he went into the signalbox he would pull out his watch to check it with the box clock. His watch was a large bulbous affair with a hinged front and back. Much pressing of levers and screwing of knobs was needed to get it to match the slow ticking box clock. It was generally acknowledged by all the staff, amidst much laughter, that, "Owd Snuffy's watch is so fuller snuff the spring wunna push the wales [wheels] round!"

If anyone else's watch stopped it was said, "You've been standing too near Owd Snuffy." He walked about in a constant cloud of snuff. A certain relief clerk used to dread being posted for holiday work at that station. He was allergic to the snuff and every time the Stationmaster went into the goods office he used to start sneezing.

Benjamin Harris was a good stationmaster, fair to his staff and interested in the running of the railway. Sale days would find him at the cattle market, a quarter of a mile from the station, talking to auctioneers, farmers, dealers and buyers to get business for the railway company.

The station had cattle pens at the dock, a string of cattle wagons and an engine to shunt the full ones out and the empty ones in. The engine stood by every sale day.

The Stationmaster with his gold buttons and gold braided cap was a popular figure and his ever-open snuff box was good for business. Many gnarled, weather-beaten fingers and thumbs dipped into the box. It was large and rectangular, made of silver and on the lid was an etched scene of a man ploughing with two Suffolk Punch horses. It was made out in great detail, including a tree and birds busily feeding on the newly turned furrows.

The box was much admired by the country folk, and strangers were often invited to, "Come and have a look at this masterpiece." It had belonged to Benjamin's late father who had been the local policeman. Before that its history was lost in time. You had only to listen for the great bursts of sneezing to locate the Stationmaster.

Many orders were taken for conveying sheep and cattle to other country stations by rail. Numbers were calculated and allocated to cattle wagons. Part loads and their prices were much argued over between the dealers and the Stationmaster, some even agreeing amongst themselves to make part loads into fully loaded wagons. After much shouting, waving of arms, pencil-sucking and writing on bits of grubby paper, agreements were reached over the railway wagons.

The next argument was over driving the flocks to the station. If two dealers got their cattle or sheep mixed on the way, chaos ensued which caused endless running about to sort out.

Many hangers-on at the sale ground were engaged by the dealers; for beer money, or more often free beer — as runners, that is to help keep the animals together on the way to the station.

One very hot summer's day, the last large flock of very obstinate sheep would not go into the pens and ran amock down the station drive. After trying to get them in for half an hour, some sheep were still loose. The men stopped by the pens, puffing and mopping their brows. They suddenly noticed one elderly man retained by the dealers lying on the railway bank. "Look at Owd Legger, 'ee's aslape", said one. Legger, in his younger days, used to push the horse-drawn canal boats through the nearby tunnel, lying on an outstretched plank from the boat, on his back and pushing with his legs against the tunnel wall. There was no towpath — the horses were led over the top.

They shouted at Legger, "Ay-up, ay-up", even went over and shook him, "Gerrup", "Comon", was demanded, but to no avail. Running about in the hot sun, combined with large quantities of strong local brewed ale known as "Brain Damage" had laid him low. They all stood around him. His breathing became quite laboured. Everyone else became quiet. The sheep had stopped their frantic baa-ing and began to graze on the railway bank.

The Driver and Fireman climbed down from the waiting engine in the sidings and came over to see what they were all looking at. Legger, his eyes tightly shut, lay motionless. "'Ee looks as if 'eesjed! [dead]", someone exclaimed. "'Ee inner movin' much", said another. "Gerra bucket er wayter an chuck ower 'im", was heartlessly suggested. They shook

Legger again, but there was no response. Alarm spread. "Way better tell Owd Snuffy." "Arr, arr", they all agreed. So the Junior Porter, known as "the Lad", was sent to Snuffy's office.

The Stationmaster was writing a letter to a farmer over a bill for hiring railway corn sacks. There was often argument over the amount owing. Sometimes the full sacks passed through two or three agents, or even another railway company, and explanations were long and tedious. A loud knocking came on the door. "Come in", said Snuffy. The door opened. The Lad stood there, puffing a bit as he had run all the way. A full blast of snuff met him. "Can yer come Mast' Arris? Summerts up wi' Owd Legger!" The Stationmaster, glad of an excuse to get away from tiresome letters, put on his gold braided hat and strode out.

As he approached the standing group, now joined by the Signalman, they parted to let him through and he gazed down on the recumbent Legger. "What's he been doing?", he asked sharply. There was silence. Then a voice from the back said, "'Ee's 'ad a belly fuller ale then run about in the 'ot sun." With that sudden burst of information they all looked at Stationmaster Harris expectantly. He in turn looked down at Legger.

He thought he had to do something. He was in charge, the leader, the man at

the wheel, the one to give the orders. They all turned to him whenever anything went wrong. He took out his snuff box to give him time to think, tapped it, opened it, took a generous pinch and drew a mighty sniff. It shot straight to his brain and enlightenment dawned — snuff, that was it!

He knelt down by the side of Legger, taking care to do so in a clean patch of grass, still holding the snuff box. Then with a thumb and forefinger loaded with a large helping of snuff, he proceeded to push it up Logger's nostrils. The snuff box lid was clicked to. He stood up and brushed the bits of loose grass off his knees. They all waited in silence.

A bell could be heard ringing in angry single strokes from the signalbox, but the Signalman could not tear himself away at that moment from the gripping drama he was witnessing. Legger's eyes flickered, he gave a little indrawn breath, then a longer one. His breathing became deeper. He gave a sniff, then another, his neck and face became a bright red, his mouth opened to take a shuddering indrawn breath allowing his top set of teeth to fall and meet the lower with a loud click.

Then, from the back of his throat it came, "Ar, ar, arrrrrr-schoooooooi." The pressure was so great that it shot his ill-fitting teeth straight up into the air to fall in the grass behind his head. "A, aa, aar, aarrr, whoooosh!" it came again.

Legger's body lifted up with the effort and thumped back on to the grass. A group of sheep that were quietly grazing nearby, jumped straight up into the air and started to hurtle about like mad things thinking someone was shooting at them!

Six times the explosions rented the air, then Legger sat bolt upright and said, "Goorrd A'mighty!" He gazed around him, looking like someone who had just had a brick dropped on his head. He licked his parched lips and suddenly realised that he had a lot of empty space in his mouth. "Me tayth! [teeth]", he cried in anguish, "Ov lost me tayth!" "Theer in the gress", he was told. "Watch out wheer yer a treading", said one, "Dunner goo and put yer gret fate on Legger's tayth."

The teeth were found, popped into his mouth, a mug of water sent for and soon Legger was pronounced fit. The Signalman went back to his ringing bells, the loco men to their engine, and the dealers to round up the stubborn sheep. Another sale day was nearly at a close. Stationmaster Benjamin Harris strode back to his office, his reputation enhanced, his status somewhat higher — an acknowledged Master of His Station.

44

The Point Oilers

THE busy shunting yard was shrouded in a cold December early morning mist. An engine propelled a string load of wagons up an incline.

A man at the top peered closely at the wagon labels in the yellow light of his paraffin hand lamp, then chalked a large number on the leading buffer. He slid his shunting pole off the buffer, under the heavy coupling chain and, with a powerful downward thrust, flipped the coupling off the hook, setting the wagon free to trundle down the incline, quickly gathering speed towards a fan of twenty different sidings which terminated at large stop blocks.

The number on the buffer was shouted down to the men working the point levers at various positions around the shunting yard.

Three coal-burning braziers near to the levers gave a welcoming glow to men trying to bring life back into numb fingers.

Wagons, vans, large and small, long and short, loomed out of the mist, rumbled by, then disappeared into the mist again, stopping with a thump and a crash further down the yard, running into stationary wagons held captive by the stop blocks.

It was as if you had stepped out of a time capsule straight into the midst of a medieval battle — the loud cries of men, brake blocks shrieking, buffers crashing, yellow flickering lights of hand lamps, the red glow of braziers, smoke from the stationary shunting engine, and eerie reflections in the mist from the open fire box door.

A man stood by a string of stationary wagons, his shunting pole hooked on to the coupling of the last wagon. He was waiting to lift the heavy chain to secure it to the hook of an oncoming wagon that loomed up out of the mist.

He braced himself and started to lift the coupling when the buffers were about six inches apart. At that moment the shunting pole slipped off the coupling, his left hand continued the upward movement and was trapped between the two buffers as they smashed together. A seering pain shot through his body, numbing his brain; he sank to the ground clutching his shattered hand.

His cries went unheard, but after a while he managed to stagger between the wagons back towards the shunters' cabin.

Fortunately one of the men on his shift was skilled in first aid. Such knowledge the Railway Company always encouraged by professional tuition and extra free passes when proficient.

A tourniquet and bandages were quickly applied. One man ran to the station to see if the early shift van driver had arrived and arranged for the injured man to be taken to the hospital with some urgency.

The surgeon could save only a small part of his forefinger and half a thumb. The rest was a fingerless stump. He would never use a shunting pole again.

Over the months that followed he came many times to see his fellow shunters. As his injuries healed, the bandages got less bulky and finally only a fingerless leather glove covered his hand.

The Railway Doctor pronounced him fit and recommended the Company to find him a light job.

To those who didn't know his name he was always referred to as "Im wi' the 'and".

Thirty years before that incident occurred a young man applied to the Railway Company for a job with the permanent way gang. He was passed fit by the Company Doctor, although thin and sparse of stature.

All went well for the first years, then spells of bronchial trouble beset him. His breathing became more and more laboured. Wielding pick and shovel, or any strenuous job in the gang became an impossibility.

The examining doctor recommended a light job be found for him. This decision coincided with the one taken on the shunter; in fact, they both sat in the same waiting room awaiting the doctors's verdict. They spoke to one another, little knowing it was the beginning of a lifelong friendship.

Anyone who couldn't remember the little platelayer's name referred to him as "Im wi' the chest".

Just outside the station a junction led off to a branch line. At the opposite end stood a locomotive depot and carriage cleaning sidings.

The whole area produced an imposing array of points and signals.

The platelayers had to clean and oil the points. Two able-bodied men spent a lot of time on this job. This left the gang shorthanded when on other essential work.

The solution to this problem was found when a light job was recommended for the ex-shunter and platelayer. The "Hand" was appointed full time point oiler, and the "Chest" his lookout man. They were quite happy to accept the job in the light of their disability.

The Chest was issued with a curved oval plate. The words "Look Out" were inscribed on it in red letters with L.M.S. over the top. Two leather straps enabled the wearer to secure it to his left arm. He was also given a red and green flag, each wound round a stout stick.

A warning horn on a long loop of cord to hang around his neck completed his equipment.

The horn was eighteen inches long, two inches wide at one end, tapering to a mouthpiece, inside which was a reed. The noise it produced when blown sounded like a cross between the call of a sheep and a donkey.

The little platelayer could manage one good blast, then had to stop to fill his tortured lungs with air. This produced a strange whistling sound within his chest. The slightest exertion always brought forth this whistling.

His mates in the gang used to say "'Ee could play a chune on them chubes if 'ee practiced." He had to take a lot of remarks about that horn. Shouts of "Ay up, 'ere's little boy blue!" "Weers yer sheep?" "Gie us a chune on yer trumpet." Ex-Army men would request, "Blow cookhouse, mate, I wants me dinner."

He took it all in good part but any requests by them to blow the horn were always met with a refusal. He would tuck it inside his jacket in a protective manner.

The lookout man had a responsible job. It was surprising how quietly a train could approach with the regulator closed. The oiler's life was in the lookout's hands, and he was never allowed to work alone.

The point oiler's equipment was a long piece of metal, flattened at one end, at the other end a smooth round knob that fitted the palm of the hand ensuring a good grip for scraping sand, ashes or coalslack out of the points, before oiling the point slides with a thick black oil, painted on with a long handled brush. The oil was carried in an open quart tin with a long wire handle.

The ex-shunter's stubby finger and thumb could just hold the oil tin and the brush, whilst his good right hand wielded the scraper. A quick change over for the brush and the points were oiled.

They got on well together from the start. The lookout man lived in the town on his own; his wife had died. The point oiler lived in the country on his own. He had never married.

They were allowed to have an old unwanted platelayer's cabin for their very own. It stood on a piece of waste ground next to a signal lamp cabin, behind a large signalbox. On one side was the high blank wall of the goods shed, on the other side was a huge stop block made of earth, tightly corseted with upright sleepers let into the ground, which in turn was bound round with a length of railway line.

The corrugated iron lamp cabin was used by a full-time lampman and his junior known as "the Lad".

They all very quickly became friends. The old cabin was cleaned out, sleeper seats made, tiles pushed back on the roof and the fireplace renovated.

The little platelayer had scrounged a large cast-iron kettle from the maintenance gang and a chipped enamel can, minus its lid, that held a gallon of drinking water. The lookout man was the tea masher; any heavier job always set his poor old "chubes a whistling".

They were outcasts in a way. Physical reasons stood them apart from their fellow workers. The lampmen were outcasts because of the paraffin! It was on their clothes and people could smell it. When they carried the full lamps it dripped down their trousers.

When they stood by a hot stove or fire their trousers gently steamed. People soon began to sniff and their eyes began to water with the paraffin vapour. Hints were dropped about the smell. NO, they definitely were not welcome.

Here in this little backwater they all stood equal together. Nobody gave a thought to the lampmen's trousers or the ex-shunter's oil-soaked trousers steaming in front of their hot fire. It was a miracle they didn't catch fire whilst sitting near a crackly, spark shooting piece of knotty sleeper wood that someone had thrown into the fire.

It was quite a pleasant job during the summer. They would stand and watch the passenger trains go hurtling by.

The little platelayer was always curious about people. "Weer thay all goin?" he would ask. "They're all a goin on theer 'olidays", was the reply from the worldly-wise point oiler. He'd been

to London once. He hadn't been outside the station, mind you, and came back on the next train, but that was further than the lookout man had been.

"Weer they all goo in the winter then?" he was asked. "They goo to see theer rich aunts and uncles and owd grannies, an folks wot can gie um theer train fare", was the reply. He had an answer for everything and the lookout man believed him.

There was only one thing he didn't have a ready answer for. It was those mysterious objects that fell from beneath the passenger trains and lay on the track on the approach to the station. They sometimes got fast in the points. His little companion tactfully never mentioned them.

The non-stop passenger trains that went roaring through were sometimes halted. Fog, mishaps, signal failure, track work and many things could slow down or on rare occasions, bring these important trains to a halt.

If one happened to stop where the point oiler and his little companion were working it became an immediate point of interest. All work was stopped and they gazed through the window and speculated upon the occupants.

"Wonder weer theer gooin?" "Weer do they cum from do ya reckon?"

If the dining car happened to stop opposite them whilst the occupants were having a meal it was even more interesting. "What do yer think theer eatin'?" "Look, they got summat in glasses, 'im in the white coat's poring it out." "Weer do ya think they gits theer money from?" "Wot do ya think 'is job is, 'im wi' the cigar?" "Wot do they want all them knives, forks and spoons for?"

They would stand on the top of the rail to get a better view. Passengers with a loaded forkful of food would suddenly be aware of two pairs of eyes looking up at them, others put their fork down and wished the train would start to move.

The two men gazed into the dining car with complete childlike innocence, not conscious of being rude or meaning to upset the diners. They looked in at a world they knew they would never be part of, like children gazing into a brightly lit toy shop with only a penny to spend.

It was on one of these occasions they were in great danger of being run down by oncoming trains because they were so absorbed by it all, and oblivious to other traffic.

When the train started to move the Hand would wave his long-handled paint brush aloft in salute, grinning up at each occupant by the window as the train slowly went past. Some stared back with a stony face, some gave a little grin, some a languid wave which only encouraged the Hand to give a bigger grin and flourish his oil brush, causing drips of oil to fall down on to his cap.

They resumed work and talked about what they had seen. "How did they cook all those meals on a train?" "Who peeled all the potatoes?" "Where did they get all the hot water from?" "Who did all the washing up?" "What did they do with the drinks left in the bottles?" "What was it like eating your dinner at 80 miles per hour?" The Chest thought it would "fill yer fuller wind at that speed!"

When they arrived back at the cabin for lunch, they told the Lampman all about the dining car in great detail.

"Little Alfie" was there too. He was the only other member of their exclusive club. He was the brake van lamp trimmer. He cleaned them out and lit the stove ready for the guards to take the freight trains out on their journeys. He had paraffin on his trousers too.

On hot days they sat in the shade of the earth stop block, on a broken wagon plank laid across some bricks. The upright sleepers round the block all leaned one way, as if cringing away from the impact of endless wagons thumping into their side.

The lookout man put his hand on the sun warmed railway line around the huge stop block. "I wunder 'ow they bent this round?" he asked. "They 'otted it up then 'ammered it round", was the ever ready reply.

On occasions a line of coaches would be backed up to the block. It was the late night train from London that terminated at the station. If the carriage cleaning sidings were full, it was shunted there until morning.

As soon as the two men came over the railway bridge they could see the coaches. The Hand came on a bicycle, the Chest walked. "Look, the coaches are in", was the excited cry. They hurried to the cabin and unlocked the door, the little lookout man puffing and panting some way behind. The Hand got a small eight-rung ladder down from where it was kept across the beams. It had been sawn off a broken ladder that had been discarded and left behind the loco shed.

He carried it round the stop block to the far side of the coaches, away from the prying eyes, and propped it up against the first coach door, then climbed up, took a T-shaped carriage key from a slot cut out of his broad leather belt, unlocked the door and climbed in.

The coaches were like the bran tub at the village garden fete. You never knew what you were going to find. Most certainly London newspapers, both daily and evening. Sometimes magazines. They liked *Picture Post* the best.

The little lookout man was an avid reader. He would put his steel-rimmed spectacles on, hook the springy side pieces round his ears, and read out bits from the newspapers to his companion when they sat in the cabin on rainy days.

He never missed *The Times* personal column, with remarks like "Cor, listen to this" or "Watter yer think this means" or "Fancy that!" "Fancy um doing that."

The magazines and papers were passed on to the other three members of their club, but always had to be put back into a large box marked "Hudson Soap", to be gone over again and again.

On one occasion an umbrella was found and the Hand generously said the Chest could have it. He was delighted and kept flicking the umbrella up and down like a toy. When he came to use it on the first wet day he appeared to have lost some of his enthusiasm. "Wot's up?" asked the Hand. "Appen," said his lookout and paused, "Appen the man wot lost it'll see it an' want it back!" he said with a worried frown. "Tell yer wot", he was told, "I got some white paint in that coco tin on the shelf wot I got off the signal painters. I'll paint the 'andle white." This was decided to be good idea and when the paint had dried the umbrella was carried without the slightest worry.

The Hand went through the first coach, sliding open each compartment door for a good look round, including under the seats; he had found half a crown there once.

His little companion was following his progress from outside, looking up at the windows, his laboured breathing whistling in his chest. "Found owt, found owt?" he asked anxiously. The first coach yielded two evening newspapers. In the rest of the train he found more newspapers, including *The Times*. That gave good value. It was a nice soft paper and after the interesting bits were read out it was kept for wrapping food in and other domestic uses. Two tea cups and two teaspoons were found and kept for use in the cabin.

Not a lot this time. They had found a straw hat and a trilby once, neither of which would fit but the Hand swapped the straw hat with a bee-keeping friend for a jar of honey.

They never found any caps. People who wore caps never seemed to leave them in the trains. Gloves sometimes came their way in winter time. A nice curved pipe once came to light in the corner of a first class compartment. That was swapped for twenty Woodbines, the Hand's favourite smoke.

It was always the thrill of what you might find that brought a little excitement into their drab lives.

The Hand always looked in the lavatories on the train. Many interesting things came to light. A discarded pair of socks, which, after turning over with his boot were left alone. Articles of ladies clothing were treated in the same way.

A man's waistcoat and tie he promptly claimed for himself, also a walking stick with a metal band around it that was thought to be silver! How could you need a stick to get on a train, then not need one to get off? they asked. It found them something to talk about as they gently steamed round the fire on wet days.

One morning, after a fruitless search through the train, he opened the lavatory door in the last coach and there hanging on a hook was a clerical collar attached to a piece of black shirt front, with tapes to tie it round the body. He took it down, opened the window at the end of the coach and threw it down to the little lookout man anxiously waiting to see if he had found anything. "Wot yer got?" "Wot's this, wot's this ere?", he said looking at the white collar and black cloth in alarm. "Put it on", was the reply, "it'll keep yer neck and chest warm."

The collar was taken back to the cabin to show the others. They all tried it on in turn, the Lampman saying to the Hand and the Chest, "I now pronounce you man and wife", amidst great laughter. The Lamp Lad put it round his neck and was told, "Yer a junior parson now so stop that swearin'!" His reply was unparson like.

They all admired themselves wearing the collar, in a broken mirror found in the carriage sidings, and wondered how it came to be left in the lavatory. "Appen ee didn't want his friends to know ee was a parson", was suggested. "Per'aps ee was going to one o' them drinking parties", said the Lampman. Little Alfie could only stare at the stiff white collar, offering no explanation at all. It was left to the Point Oiler to have the last word. "Ee must a been a'goin' to meet a woman an' chucked 'is collar away", he said with great conviction.

The collar and black material were hung on a nail in the cabin, the subject of speculation for many weeks to come.

A small window was let into the large blank expanse of the woodwork at the rear of the signalbox. It overlooked the oiler's cabin. The signalman often peered out, looking down to see what they were doing. But there was no friendly wave or smile; the gap in rank was too wide. It was a look of curiosity, especially when the delicious aroma of cooking wafted up to the signalbox.

The Hand did all the cooking; he was a bachelor and was used to looking after himself. The little lookout man had fared badly since his wife had died. He had very little skill in the kitchen and welcomed the meals in the cabin.

In the long summer days they would sometimes have two cooked meals a day. The food wouldn't keep too long so at lunch time out would come the frying pan or saucepan from the tea chest which was fitted with a stout wooden lid to keep inquisitive mice at bay, and soon sizzlings and bubblings were heard in the cabin and a lovely smell would waft across the railway lines.

When they finished work at five o'clock, neither of them had any urgent reason to dash off home, so any surplus perishable food was cooked and a late meal eaten in the cabin, thus saving much bother when they got home. Besides, the coal was free at the cabin. They picked their own coal from the spillage in the shunting yard. None was ever issued.

Sausage, liver, black pudding, bacon, eggs, tripe and great pans of onions were eaten. All were much favoured and easily prepared. On meatless days, chips were cooked in a large blackened saucepan, in dripping kept in a glazed earthenware pot that had once held plum jam.

When money was short they had to make do with toast and dripping or fried cheese and onions. They usually found something to cook and with large mugs of tea it was the high spot of the day.

The Hand often talked about taking the Chest on a trip to London. He considered himself a seasoned traveller, having made the trip once. On the strength of that his little companion

eventually agreed. "Beein' as you know 'ow to goo on", he said, "we'll goo."

Free passes were applied for and the great day arrived. It had to be on a Sunday; it was the only day they were off together.

The two travellers met on the platform with plenty of time to spare, to catch the ten o'clock train.

They eyed one another up and down. Apart from meeting in the doctor's waiting room, they had only seen each other in working clothes. "You're all toffed up", said the Hand. The little lookout man wore wide-bottomed flannels, a dark blazer with metal buttons, a white shirt and collar and a tie with coloured stripes running diagonally across. The collar was speared through with a polished tie pin, all topped off with a trilby hat. His late wife had chosen every item and thought the trilby made him look taller.

He brushed imaginary specks off his sleeve and said apologetically, "I 'aven't 'ad it on for a long time." He paused. "You 'er, you look quite 'er, smart", he said, gazing at the point oiler, who was wearing a new pair of railway trousers saved from his shunting days, a black jacket and waistcoat that had once belonged to his Uncle Joe, long since dead, and from the same source a black cap with a button on top, sewn together in segments. The raised seams making it look like a cake cut into slices, the button on the top being the cherry. A large peak jutted out, defying even the strongest sun to ever get near the wearers eyes.

He wore a striped flannel shirt with a white celluloid collar, held together with a large stud front and back. The stud at the front had already made an angry red mark on his Adam's apple, all tightly bound round with a thin black railway issue tie. A new leather fingerless glove covered his left hand. In his good hand he clutched a large brown paper parcel.

"Let's walk up to the front", he said "Wes' all get a better seat there." They walked towards the end of the platform. Soon the train roared in and stopped with the shrieking of brake blocks.

Sure enough, near the engine was an empty compartment. They quickly boarded the train, slid the door open and sat in the window seats.

Soon the train was off, and after admiring the framed pictures of Llandudno and Colwyn Bay behind the seats, they gazed out of the window in eager anticipation of sights to see, like two children on their first train journey.

They sat enthralled, each one speaking to the other on the points of interest. "Look theer!" "See that?" "Look at that" "What's that?" "Ther's a boat on the canal!"

A passenger train hurtled by on the adjoining line and startled them. "Cor, that was close! It's a good job we 'adn't got our 'eads out!"

Further down the coach a loud voice was heard shouting something about tickets. "It's the ticket mon!" said the Chest, instantly producing his ticket. Very soon the compartment door was flung open with a crash and a large man stood in the doorway. "Your tickets!" he shouted, he paused, adding as an after thought, "If you please."

The letters in gold braid on his cap bore the dreaded words 'Ticket Inspector'. Everything about him shone and twinkled. Lights flashed from his buttons and the peak of his cap. A chain hanging from his lapel to his pocket watch, and a shorter one to his whistle, would have done credit to a guardsman on duty outside Buckingham Palace. His black trousers with red piping down the sides had knife-edge creases. Boot toe caps were polished to mirrored perfection, the secret known only to military men proficient in the use of the hot spoon and candle, ironing every imperfection out of the surface of the leather. In his other lapel a red rose, flanked by two symmetrical green leaves, matching the exact colour of the red piping on his jacket.

He wore a tight celluloid collar and black railway tie. His face red and a hairless neck overhung the collar at the back. It was pitted with small craters, like extinct volcanos, that suggest terrible suffering in some far flung part of the Empire. A generous nose overhung a clipped bristly moustache.

In his right hand he held a pair of ticket nippers polished to a silver-sheen with red knife polish scrounged from the dining car staff.

"Tickets ... if you please!", he shouted again. The Chest held his out. It was scrutinised intently, then a piece was nipped out of it with the gleaming instrument, and handed back.

He turned to the Hand who had been gazing at some lineside houses. The train was travelling up an embankment so he was able to look down into some of the rooms and observe the Sunday morning activities.

Many were still in bed with tightly drawn curtains. Some sat round the breakfast table, others read the paper. One couple appeared to be shouting at one another waving their arms around.

A man in pyjamas stared back at him and the Hand, being a friendly chap, waved to him.

He finally tore himself away from the window and began to search for his ticket. First in one pocket, then another. His jacket, waistcoat, trousers, all pockets tried but in vain. Even his left hand with his stubby thumb and finger fumbled ineffectively in his pockets to try and help with the search.

The little lookout man looked on with growing alarm, his breath whistling in his chest. He said urgently, "Let me look! Let me look! Old yer 'ands up!" His companion held his hands high in the air, as though at the point of a pistol, whilst a second search was made of his pockets.

The ticket inspector clicked his ticket nippers impatiently and pursed his lips. The bristles of his moustache stuck straight out pointing at the Hand as if ready to be fired into him like deadly arrows.

"We're both railwaymen", the little man gasped, "we oil the points up at the junction and 'ee busted his 'and a'tween the buffers when 'ee was a shunter." He poured the words out hoping it would extract a spark of friendliness from the waiting Inspector. But it was not to be.

"Oh yerrse", was the reply, "well you've still got to 'ave a ticket or pay me!" His left hand went to the brass whistle stamped "The Acme Thunderer" like a cowboy going for his gun, as if to stop the train immediately and have the Hand thrown off.

This brought forth more pleas from the Chest. "Ee's got a ticket, ee's got one. I've seen it", he wheezed, "wot 'ave yer done with it? Where 'ave yer put it?", he implored his friend who still stood quite calmly with his hand in the air, looking up at the carriage roof as if deep in thought.

Suddenly and dramatically, the point oiler spoke. "Owd yer! Owd yer!" He lowered his arms and bent his head; the Ticket Inspector thinking he was about to be attacked took a step backward. But no, the cap was gently removed from his head and inside, lying on the large shelf-like peak, were two pieces of half smoked Woodbine cigarettes, a match and the illusive ticket.

The two were all smiles now. "I told yer 'ee 'ad a ticket! I told yer! I knew I'd put it safe somewhere"; they both spoke together.

But the Ticket Inspector only scowled. He held the ticket by the extreme corners, giving him the least contact with it, as though it was contaminated with the most deadly disease.

He read every detail on it, front and back, even holding it to the light, as if trying to detect a near perfect forgery. He darted glances at them from his black button eyes.

It went quiet in the compartment. The little lookout man was holding his breath, his wheezing had stopped.

The ticket was slowly placed in the shining nipper jaws, even then he hesitated, still hoping to find some defect in the piece of thick cardboard and prolonging the agony for the two watchers. Suddenly, a squeeze, a click and it was done. A vee-piece was nipped out of the ticket and it was handed back to the Hand.

The Ticket Inspector went towards the door, stopped, turned round and fixed them with a malevolent gaze. His bristling moustache appeared to be ready for firing at them again. They instinctively drew closer together.

"In future", he growled, "you want to have your tickets 'andy, it saves a lotta time." And with that parting shot he crashed the compartment door to and was gone.

They looked at each other in silence. Then the Chest spoke, "Cor, I didn't like 'im, did you?", he asked. "Nar, I didn't", answered his companion, who was examining his ticket and was tenderly feeling the spot where the Ticket Inspector had cut a piece out of it. "Ee's chomped a bit outer me ticket", he said indignantly, "ee didn't oughter a done that, being as I'm a Railway man same as 'im."

Free pass tickets were usually left unmarked so the owners could continue to use them again right up to the expiry date. "We could 'a come a 'gen wi' this ticket if he'd left it a' be instead er 'acking at it wi' them nippers", he complained bitterly.

The Hand was proper put out and it was some time before he calmed down and put the ticket back into the shelf-like compartment inside his cap.

He started to put the things back into his pockets that had been taken out during the search for the ticket. A packet of Wild Woodbine cigarettes, a large shut-knife, a nail, a piece of string, a handkerchief with some coins tied in one corner, a small stone with a hole through the middle that he had found in his garden and was convinced it would bring him luck, and protect him from evil things he knew not what; a flat tin that had once contained fiery throat lozenges, now filled with strong flat peppermints, and finally a "Tommy" spoon.

A "Tommy" would open any toilet door on any station, without having to part with the traditional penny. You first had to acquire a railway teaspoon, all nicely embossed with the Company's initials of course.

That was easy. They were left on window ledges, in corners, in empty carriages, often still by the tea cups, by travellers either in haste to get on or to get off the trains.

They were also found lying on the track. The Hand declared, "They must a' been chucked out wi' the washing up water", thrown from the dining car kitchen.

The spoon was laid on the rail, the bowl end hammered flat, then rubbed on the sandstone buttress of the railway bridge to grind it down to the size and shape of a penny. You now had a penny with a handle, so to speak.

When the flat end was inserted into the penny slot at the top of the large brass lock on the toilet door, it released the bolt and the door would open.

The penny was then pulled out ready for the next time. It was an ever-lasting toilet penny and you could also stir the tea with it! Tommy Crapper would have been annoyed, had he been there, to see his famous brain child being used free of charge. The Railway Company would have also been outraged had they know about the practice — and their own spoons too! It just goes to show, if it is necessary, it will get invented.

They had been travelling through the suburbs for some time, gradually reducing speed, and very soon stopped with a jerk in the very heart of the capital itself — London!

"We're 'ere", cried the Hand and clutching his brown paper parcel he opened the door and ushered his companion out on to the platform.

They stood there like two rocks, letting the tide of people sweep past them, to empty into the street in the frantic search for cabs or buses or, for some, a different platform, another train.

The little lookout man gazed at the huge domed roof. "Cor look at that roof", he cried, throwing his head right back to take it all in. He nearly overbalanced and the Hand led him to an empty seat on the platform, out of the way of the rushing passengers. They both sat there, lost for words, looking all around at the vast amount of information the station offered to the

venturesome travellers.

Large wooden boards faced with iron letters hung from the roof, others stuck straight out from the walls, giving information or directions to anxious upturned faces:

WAITING ROOM, REFRESHMENT ROOM, DINING ROOM, COLD LUNCHEON AND TEA BASKETS, GENTLEMEN, LADIES ROOM, LEFT LUGGAGE, TICKET OFFICE, BOOKING HALL, PARCELS OFFICE, TELEGRAPH OFFICE.

A large cast iron finger with a clenched fist pointed in the direction of OUT.

Higher up the wall a varied assortment of vitreous enamelled signs in all colours, pleaded mutely to be noticed:

VIROL, STEPHEN'S INK, EARLES CEMENT, EPP COCOA, PEARS SOAP, HUDSON SOAP, DRUMMER DYES, ROWNTREES COCA, COLMANS MUSTARD, RECKITTS BLUE, ROBIN STARCH, ZEBRA BLACK LEAD, VAN HOUTEN'S COCOA, BOVRIL, TEA ROSE & WHITE ROSE, AMERICAN LAMP OILS. CHURCHMANS NOTED SHAG. PACKETS ONLY, THE BEST LASTS LONGER. Mr Palethrop even had his sausages illustrated in coloured enamel in a bid to tempt customers.

As you ascended the station footbridge, MAZAWATEE TEA on blue and yellow enamel plates were screwed to every stair riser. They flashed before your eyes with every upward step.

Trains came, trains went. Parcels, boxes, mailbags, newspapers, luggage, was all loaded up, whistles blown, flags waved, and away they went. Minutes later, another arrived, and seemingly all was unloaded again.

They sat quite enthralled, like two children on a seaside outing. Suddenly the Chest spoke, "I'm 'ungry an' I forgot to bring anything." The Hand grinned and said, "It's a good job I remembered then." He unwrapped the brown paper parcel. Inside were four sugar bags made of thick blue paper. Three contained sandwiches, some with black pudding, some with cheese. The fourth bag was full of small cooked potatoes, complete with salt in a screw of paper.

He generously shared them with his companion and they both sat munching contentedly.

Four pigeons swooped down from some place high in the domed roof and landed about a yard from their feet. They walked confidently up to them and started to peck at fallen crumbs. They looked well fed but a bit grimy.

On a four-wheeled station barrow nearby were four baskets of racing pigeons. They could be heard gently cooing and muttering to one another between trains.

The Hand made a profound statement: "It's a funny owd world", he said and

paused. "Them pigeons there", he nodded towards the ones pecking by his feet, "live a grand life. No wind er rain to bother 'em. Plenty er people about to feed 'em, plenty er water to drink in them fire buckets over there. No wonder they're as fat as a butcher's dog. But them pigeons there", he pointed dramatically at the baskets on the barrow, "'ave got to flap their guts out fer 'undreds of miles afore they even get a crumb to eat!"

The Chest looked up at the girdered roof then at the pigeons by his feet, then at the pigeons in the baskets. He swivelled his head round and repeated the process. "Ar", he agreed, "yer right."

He went over to the pigeon baskets and peered at the label. "Cor", he said, "they've come from Yorkshire an' are gooin' to be let out at Brighton!" He bent down and applied one eye to a small aperture in the wickerwork. A small bright, intelligent, unwinking eye stared back at him. They surveyed one another for a few seconds. The Chest spoke to the eye — "YOU 'VE GOTTER LONG WAY TO GO ME OWD BOD AFORE YER GET 'OME. I'LL GET YER SOME BREAD IF THEAR'S ANY LEFT."

He went back to the seat muttering to himself. "Yorkshire — Ow will they find their way back theer?"

The Hand heard him and gave him the answer immediately.

"Magnetic, it's the magnetic."

"Wot?"

'It's the magnetic wot does it."

"Magnetic?"

"Ar."

"Is that like, er, the electric'?"

"Well, er, ar, a bit."

Silence fell. The Chest stood holding a crust of bread and looking at his companion who went on to explain.

"When them pigeons all get together in the loft where they live back 'ome, it gets full of magnetic from their bodies, cos they're all 'appy and contented. So when they're flying 'igh in the sky, they can feel the magnetic pull on their beaks and 'eads, so it guides 'um 'ome."

The Chest digested this revelation for a while, then said "Wot do they fly round and round for then when they're first let out?"

"It's to find the magnetic pull on their beaks and 'eads. They don't feel it on their backside. It's a good job they don't", said the practical Hand, "or they would be a flapping backwards wouldn't they?"

They looked at each other. No titter, smirk or smile crossed their faces. Why should it? The Hand believed it to be true because his father had believed it and told him all about it.

"Fancy that", said the Chest in amazement, "I allus wondered 'ow they did it."

He went back to the basket and pushed the crumbled bread through the wickerwork, then bent down to look through the hole again, subjecting the pigeons to a searching stare. They stared back at him. He was seeing them in an entirely new light.

The Hand said he was, "parchin' for a drink", so off they went to a little place on the end of Number One Platform, where they sold tea and coffee. It was a one-room affair with a partition down the middle, with one entrance from outside the station, used by cab drivers waiting for customers. The platform side was mostly used by railwaymen.

Two large pot mugs of tea were enjoyed. The Chest bought two thick jam sandwiches and two thick cheese sandwiches. He asked if they could be wrapped up please, and the lady behind the counter obliged, thus ensuring sustenance on their journey home.

Strolling down the platform a little later, the Hand guided his little companion to a large box-like contraption standing by the wall. It was a heavy iron die-stamping machine which produced embossed letters on an aluminium strip, twelve letters for a penny. He had been shown how to work this machine on his previous trip to the station. He hadn't told the Chest and wanted it to be a surprise.

"Wot is it? Wot does it do?" he was asked. "I'll show yer, I'll wok 'er for yer", he proudly replied.

Bridlington

GUIDE FREE FROM INFORMATION BUREAU BRIDLINGTON OR ANY L·N·E·R AGENCY

Inserting a penny he selected a letter and banged the handle. After repeating this a number of times a strip of metal emerged from the machine which he handed triumphantly to his watching companion, who, on looking at the embossed letters, said with surprise, "Why, that's me name!"

They both grinned with delight then decided that the Hand's name should be stamped out on the machine as well, and that they would nail both names on their cabin door at the Junction.

Further down the platform, coloured posters were on display depicting all the delights of the seaside. They stood gazing at a poster of Scarborough with a clear blue sky. A young man with a thin moustache, white trousers and black jacket, sat by a glamourous young lady wearing a check skirt and white blouse, on a cliff top overlooking the bay. On the grass beside them was a pair of binoculars, a packet of Gold Flake cigarettes, a box of chocolates and a box camera.

It painted an idyllic picture. But they liked the Bridlington poster best. A man was trying to row a boat off the beach. But it was impossible. Why? you ask. Because the boat was full of girls in bathing costumes, the sea was full of girls, the beach was full of girls.

He couldn't swing the oars for fear of bashing some poor girl on the head or knocking them out of the boat. A dog swimming out in front seemed in danger of being run down as well.

They counted twenty-two bathing belles in the poster, and only two men. Yes, they definitely liked that one the best.

"We oughter 'ave a day at the sea", said the Chest wistfully. "Ar, we 'ad", the Hand agreed.

They finally had to tear themselves away from the poster in order to catch the train home.

They walked right up to the top of the platform to be near the engine. The 'Hand' had already enquired about the time and platform from two railway officials, but he wanted to ask the driver just to make sure. "Bein' as 'e knows best", he said.

The train came in. The Hand was reassured by the driver that it was the right train, so they climbed aboard and soon were off.

They had to share a compartment on the way back home.

They got a friendly smile from the guard when he came to inspect the tickets. No pieces clipped out this time.

The two intrepid travellers got off the train and parted on the platform amid cries of, "See yer in the mornin'." "Ar see yer in the mornin'." "Appen the coaches 'ull be in." "Ar, they might."

The Hand went to get his cycle from the cabin and set off for home.

What tales they would have to tell about their day's outing. The lost ticket, the Ticket Inspector, the pigeons, the posters. They would all be told many times.

The ticket — he had kept it of course — and the embossed name plates would be passed around the little select group — Lampman, the Lad and Little Alfie, as they all gently steamed in front of the hot fire in the point oiler's cabin.

Lamp Out!

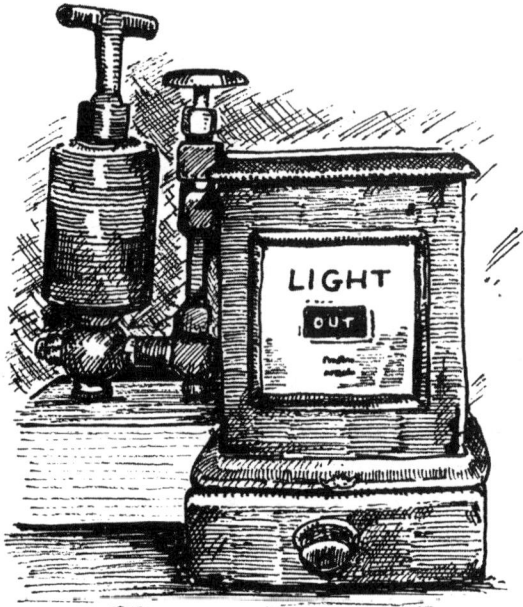

IT was a wet, cold windy night. The Signalman hung two sacks either side of the signalbox door on the conveniently placed nails. Then a rolled-up sack along the bottom in an effort to stop some of the draught that whistled through the ill-fitting door. He wedged the sliding windows with pieces of wood to stop them rattling, hung the handlamp on the back of the locker, picked up his copy of the *Beano* and was all set to have a good read.

He lay with his head on a rolled-up fogman's overcoat and his feet close to the stove which was roaring away, bringing a red glow to the cast-iron chimney pipe. It wasn't long before his eyes closed, the *Beano* dropped from his hands and snores were competing with the howling wind.

He started to dream about the nice lady porter who appeared to be calling from the end of the platform. He tried to get to her, but every step was like walking on broken glass. By this time the heat from the stove had melted the soles of his slippers and the box was filled with smell of burning rubber.

The Signalman's dream was rudely interrupted by the harsh buzzing from the block shelf. He opened his eyes, sat up and looked wildly around him. He became aware of burning pains in his feet and tried to kick off his slippers, but they had stuck to the lino. His stockinged foot caught the cast-iron tray surrounding the stove and he held his toe, hopping up and down. Unfortunately his other foot, now out of the other slipper, hoped on to a sharp piece of coal. "Aaagh! Oooh!" His shouts were enough to lift the roof off. The instrument on the block shelf was still buzzing, and beside it a small wooden box with a glass window displayed the dreaded word "OUT". To add insult to injury the down distant light signal lamp was showing "out". He turned a switch and silence descended.

He rubbed his injured foot for a while, then gave two on the bell to the box in the rear, and hobbled to the phone. It took more goes on the bell before the other signalman came to the phone. "Wossup, wossup?" – he didn't sound pleased. "Me down distant's out", came the reply. There was a silence for a second. "Down distant out? Bloody down distant out? Are you sure?" "Arr, it's buzzin' all the while." "Oo trimmed the lamp?" "The morning man, ee allus' turns the wick too 'igh, then a lump er soot drops on the wick and out it goes. I'd like to light a battern er straw under 'is bed and soot 'im up." "That means I've gotter stop and warn every bloody train tonight", said the other signalman. "Ah well we'll have ter put it in the book and I'll tell control, right?" They

hung up and sat on their lockers to curse their luck.

The first train to be cautioned was a fully fitted freight. It could be heard whistling furiously at the sight of the distant signal showing caution. It was still raining and blowing as the signalman put on his coat, overcoat, scarf and cap, and having brought the train nearly to a stand at the home signal, pull it off, picked up the handlamp, walked down the steps to show a red light. The train ground to halt at the signalbox.

Two heads popped out of the cab to enquire "Wossup?" "The next distant signal is out, go at caution", was the reply. "Distant out, distant out?" the driver shouted, "you must put water in the lamps round 'ere. It's time they took the roof off the signalboxes and chopped the bloody lockers up to liven you up a bit." He pointed at the box where the red glow from the fire shone out. "You've got a fire in there that would steam an engine for five miles!" With that parting shot he blew off his brakes and jerked the regulator open, making the wheels slip like mad.

The signalman went back up the box steps and watched the train go by. The guard was standing on the verandah of his brake, holding his watch and pointing from it to the signalman blaming him for the loss of time. The signalman responded by making certain gestures with his fingers.

The next eight trains until daylight all had to be stopped and cautioned, subjecting the signalman to more sarcasm and blasphemy. It was suggested that the signalman couldn't run a Hornby railway, and another said that it was a good job he didn't work in a lighthouse or he'd have all the bloody ships on the rocks! The reply was, "It's a good job you 'avn't got to steer your engine or you'd be off the road before you'd gone many yards."

At the other box, 0600 came and with it the morning signalman. He was told about the lamp out and all the abuse the other signalman had taken. A new lamp was promised for the distant signal and the night man went home.

When the junior porter, known as "the Lad", came to the box from the station he was given a newly trimmed and lit lamp with the orders, "You can take this down distant as soon as you can and DON'T let the Stationmaster see you bring one back." Later that morning the Lad came back with the offending lamp. On opening the door it was found to have been smoking and a lump of soot

had fallen on the flame and extinguished it. "You shudder turned it down! You shunt 'er turned it so 'igh", protested the Lad. They eventually called a truce and the signalman set about cleaning the lamp.

All the soot was removed from the glass sides and lamp top. The burner was cleaned, the wick trimmed, and all the paraffin poured out of the vessel which was then refilled. The wick was lit and the lamp placed on the top of the lamp cupboard to burn until the end of the shift. At 2 p.m. the signalman blew the lamp out, and tied a label to it which read "Failed lamp for examination, Signal and Telegraph dept., Derby". The truth was the lamp should have been sent to Derby exactly as it came from the signal, but the signalman would have been blamed. It was always a mystery to the boffins at Derby why some failed lamps were in such pristine condition!

On the report where it read "In your opinion what was the cause of the failed lamp?". The signalmen presented a united front and wrote "The wind blowed it out".

They heard no more about it!

The Stationmaster's Trousers

TWO platelayers were tightening bolts on the fishplate near the end of the platform. The Stationmaster appearing on the station, walked over and stopped beside them. They ignored him and carried on tightening the bolts. He cleared his throat, "I, er." They looked up. "I wondered if you could empty 'IT' one night?"

They looked at him in silence. It was the only occasion he ever spoke to them.

"It is rather full", he said.

Albert, one of the larger platelayers said, "Ar, we'll do 'er."

The Stationmaster still lingered. He cleared his throat again, "I wonder", he said, "if you could take it further down the garden and put it in smaller holes?"

Albert took out his pipe, spat on the ballast and said, "Ar, we'll do that then."

The Stationmaster nodded and walked back to his office.

It was a country station built in the

1870s with three flush toilets and one in the Stationmaster's house. It was miles away from any main drainage, so they all emptied into a brick-lined pit in the Stationmaster's garden, flushed with water hand-pumped by the Porter from a well up to a tank in the roof every morning.

The Porter was very proud of his water closets. He often talked about them to the villagers in his local tavern. They were amazed, never having seen one and couldn't understand with all that rushing water how you didn't get your feet wet!

Farm hands from outlying hamlets visiting the station with horse and cart for the first time were often given a conducted tour.

PORTER: "Come and 'ave a look at me water closets!"

FARM HAND: (looking down into the pan), "It aint very big, is it? 'er'll soon get full."

PORTER: "Corse it won't, it empties every time!"

FARM HAND: "I only empties mine once a week."

PORTER: "This empties out of the bottom."

FARM HAND: (pointing into the pan) "Well 'er must be bunged up then, that water ain't gooing away."

PORTER: (getting annoyed that anyone should criticise his closets pulled the chain.)

FARM HAND: (amazed) "Wheer's that goo then?"

PORTER: "It goos in the Stationmaster's garden."

FARM HAND: (face brightening) "Ar, that's clever, I 'ave to carry mine."

The Porter reluctantly closed the door and went about his duties, the farm hand to his horse and cart.

The platelayers didn't have to empty "IT". They did it because he paid them, and if they didn't do it no one else would, so he had to be a bit careful about asking them.

Two nights later at 10 p.m. with all the station house windows tightly shut, Albert and his mate arrived, armed with two lanterns, two long-handled ladles, wearing old clothes, and pushing a wheelbarrow each, ready to empty "IT".

Taking off the cover, Albert remarked, "AR, 'ers full alright." It was, right up to the overflow pipe that led straight to the nearby canal.

The last time they had emptied "IT" they were in a hurry and dug a large deep hole near to the pit, ladled it in, covered it and left. A week later the Stationmaster walking across the garden, broke through the crust and floundered knee deep in the hole.

The platelayers would never have found that out, but for the woman from the village who did some cleaning at the Station house. She saw the trousers in a bucket of water. The Stationmaster's

wife explained and said, "If you could do anything with them, then take them away." The cleaner said she could and would thank you. So for many years her husband went to church in the Stationmaster's trousers.

Albert laughed loud and long when he heard the story, he said he had a better claim to the trousers than the cleaner's husband and always told him so when he saw him out on a Sunday.

They dug four holes at the far end of the garden, then ladled the contents of the pit into the barrows, wheeled them to the holes and tipped it in.

After two hours it was empty, they put the cover back on and went home to bed, remembering their wive's strict instructions about leaving their clothes in the out-house.

Two days later the Porter handed them a sealed envelope each containing a half-a-crown, thus ensuring good will for the next time.

The Stationmaster's guests from the town often remarked about the quality and taste of his garden produce. Ignorance certainly was bliss, and Angels did not go treading in that garden!

The Fogmen

THE signalmen peered out of the window into a frosty foggy night. The frozen droplets sparkled on the handrails around the signalbox, lit by the yellow light from an oil lamp in the cast-iron lamp post at the bottom of the steps.

Sometimes he thought the fog was lifting, then at other times he was sure it was getting thicker. He looked at the large pendulum clock over the desk: it said 11.30 p.m. Suddenly he made up his mind and went to the instrument shelf. At one end stood a large brass bell push above which was a brass bell with the ringing clapper on the outside marked "L. & N.W. Rly". A handwritten card at the side said:

Call attention .... 1 long ring.
Come to signalbox ... 2 long rings.
Fogmen required ...... 3 long rings.
Testing .... 16 long rings.

He pressed the bell push for about thirty seconds, then stood back. He was committed now, no going back. He waited for two minutes then gave it an even longer push; another wait, another push, his eyes glued to the bell clapper as though willing it to start wagging, but it was no good, it was dead. He flicked it with his finger making it ping once. It was alive at this end; it was the other end that was dead.

He peered out of the window again,

cupping his hand round his eyes. He could see that the fog was definitely getting thicker.

He spoke on the telephone to the signalmen on either side of his box, then with a heavy sigh took off his slippers, put on his boots, jacket, overcoat, hat, scarf, gloves, picked up the hand lamp and went out into the freezing fog, down the long station drive and out through the gates to a row of four isolated railway cottages.

The Signalman went through the gate of the first cottage, past the fowl pen, rabbit hutches and a stack of split sleeper wood. A dog shot out of an old barrel used as a kennel, barking and growling as if to tear him to pieces, his eyes shining red in the light of the hand lamp. The Signalman had been round before and knew the reach of his chain, but prayed that it wouldn't snap with the furious onslaught. He knocked on the door and waited.

The fog gently swirled and ice twinkled on the surface of the water in the rain barrel by the door. His fingers were frozen and he tried to warm them on the top of the hand lamp, but it only brought the smell of scorched wool to his nostrils. A movement behind the bedroom window caught his eye, then a fist was thumped on the window frame. It was reluctant to open; parts of it had swelled tight with the wet, other places had large gaps that were packed tight with any material to hand.

After much thumping and banging, the window flew open, showering the upturned face of the Signalman with bits of paper, rags and strips of ladies' stockings that had been very effective in keeping the draughts out of the platelayer's bedroom.

A face peered out, wearing a cap. He must either have slept in it or kept it at his bedside. "What's up Dad?" ("Dad" did not mean any blood relation; it was a common greeting of the time.)

"I've been ringing your bell", the Signalman replied.

"Er anna rung 'ere, Dad", the face said. The Signalman knew why it hadn't rung. The bell over the platelayer's bed was stuffed full of paper! Years before, when he was a lot younger, the platelayer didn't mind night calls and the extra money, but now, nearing retirement, he wasn't very keen.

"Shall you call the fogmen, Abe?" the Signalman said.

"Ar, or-reet", was reluctantly drawn from Abraham the Platelayer. The dog was still barking and, with its collar pulled tight at the end of the chain, seemed in danger of strangulation until a loud, "Shurrup an' gerrin that tub", from Abe sent it back into the barrel, bitterly disappointed that he never even tasted a piece of the Signalman's trousers.

A woman's voice from the bedroom

was heard angrily to say, "Shut that winder, it's perishing in 'ere." The window was thumped back a few times to get it to close. The Signalman turned away and walked back along the path. This set the dog barking again. He ignored it and went back to the signalbox, stamping his feet to try to bring back some warmth into them.

As he approached the box he could hear the bells and telephone ringing and he knew it was going to be one of those nights. He hated the fog. In the distance the dog was still barking.

Abe had to cycle a mile to the village to call two other platelayers for fogging duties. Two for the distant signals, and one for the outer home signal. It would be a while before they arrived at the signalbox so the Signalman settled down to work the trains "double block" until the fogmen were at the signals.

At half-past midnight, Abe clumped up the steps, opened the box and said, "Arve towd um Dad." His eyebrows were rimy with frost. He moved to the stove where the bottom of the chimney pipe glowed cherry red. "Ers a cowd 'un terneet." His slight frame was padded out with clothes. Over his overcoat he wore a sack bag, his head through a hole cut in the middle; half the sack down his front, half down his back, secured all around with a piece of tarred string from a wagon sheet.

As the hot stove melted the frost on the sack, letters appeared proclaiming "Bibby's Cattle Food" in green letters, and beneath "Calf Starter Meal". He untied the string, unbuttoned layers of coats down to a cord waistcoat, exposing a steel chain arising from a deep pocket. He pulled up the chain, winding it around his fingers, like a ship pulling up anchor. Fastened to the end of the chain was a flat, shiny tin, the letters long worn off, the lid tied down with a piece of snare wire. Undoing the wire and flipping the lid open revealed what looked like a round mummy swathed in bandages. Unwrapping the rags eventually brought to light a pocket watch with the word "Ingersol" written across the face.

He gazed at the watch intently, rubbing the glass, then at the signalbox clock, he suddenly pointed at the clock and said dramatically, "Er's ten minutes slow, Dad!" The box clock was checked with a time signal by phone every morning at 9:00 a.m. and it never varied more than half a minute. The Signalman, who had witnessed the unveiling of Abe's watch many times before, said sarcastically, "I'd better send for a replacement clock then."

"Ar, yer want to, Dad", replied Abe in all seriousness.

He started to wind up the watch, holding the winding knob stationary in his left hand, while he turned the body of the watch backward and forward with his right hand. It sounded like sawing wood. Mr. Ingersol would have winced had he been present. He gave it one last look, then interred the watch back in the tin, then into the depths of his pocket. "Ah'll goo and get the 'and lamps out o' the cabin", he said.

The clock now said one o'clock in the morning.

He came back to the signalbox a few minutes later clutching three hand-lamps and lined them up on top of the lamp cupboard. Then he opened the fronts of the lamps, pulled out the middle holding in the coloured glasses, removed the burners and peered into the vessels. "They're all boone dry", he exclaimed, as if making a remarkable discovery, "there inner a dropper ile in any on 'um."

The Signalman knew quite well, and so did Abe, there was never any paraffin left in the fogman's headlamps; any surplus was used to make the sticks burn more fiercely under the cast-iron kettle the first morning back to normal duties in the cabin.

The Signalman opened the lamp cupboard door and took out a small can with a curved narrow spout and put it next to the lamps. "Mind that", he said, "it's full right up."

"Ar", said Abe, and started to fill the vessels. The first stream of paraffin missed the hole completely and went all over the top of the lamp cupboard. The second attempt filled the small vessel so fast that it overflowed over the sides. Abe looked out of the corner of his eye at the Signalman who was watching. "Er's swellkerd ower a bit. Dad", he said, apologetically. He was handed a bundle of cotton waste without a word.

Voices were heard outside and soon feet clumped up the signalbox stairs. The other two fogmen had arrived. The door opened and in came Joseph. "Cor, this frost gets right inter me boones", was his first remark, as he headed straight for the red glow of the stove. He was well padded beneath his railway overcoat, a scarf around his ears and a cloth cap well down over his eyes. His head was tucked in a corner of a sack, which hung down his back advertising "Silcocks Horse Nuts" in red letters. A leather belt with a large brass buckle stopped the garment from flapping about.

Behind Joseph came the third fogman, Ruben. He looked quite smart in his farmer's leggings and deerstalker hat with the flaps down over his ears. His wife had brought them at the Vicar's jumble sale held in the church room in aid of the crumbling stonework in the ancient tower.

"Ay up me owd bod", said Ruben, "this owd rimy frost dunna afe stick to yer." He carefully placed a clean washed flour sack in the corner of the signalbox. As he let go of the neck, it emitted a

peculiar squeaking noise. The
Signalman heard it and said sharply,
"You haven't got that melodian again,
have you?"

Ruben grinned and said, "Ar, it wunna
'urt nowt."

Ruben was an accomplished
performer on the melodian, as had been
his father. He was in great demand at
weddings, parties, or at the local tavern.
He liked weddings the best as there
was always, well nearly always, plenty
of food and drink and Ruben had long
staying power in both these fields.

He could keep playing without
repetition into the early hours, but
eventually time would find him lying on
the floor, especially if he had been
drinking "Owd Granny Birkett's Parsnip
Wine". He would still have his melodian
clasped across his chest, still playing
mark you, but once he stopped playing
in that position, his eyes would close
and he was done. It was no good saying
"Come on, Ruben, give us a last tune."
Even shaking him did no good. Ruben
had played his last tune that night, or
more like that morning. They either
threw a coat over him where he was, or
pushed him home on Pincher Martin's
handcart.

Ruben's only rival was Billy Thrush,
known as "Fiddler Thrush", because
he was always trying to scrape tunes
on an old fiddle. Fiddler worked with
the gang on the local canal. Often the

organiser of a party would ask both Fiddler and Ruben to play at the same function out of sheer mischief. They would start playing together and all would be well for a while, but soon remarks like, 'Yo anna gotter rate", or, "Er dunna goo like that", would be hurled about. It usually ended with Ruben and his supporters at one end of the room and Fiddler Thrush with his followers at the other, each bellowing the same song in a different key, or even a different song, each musician trying to play louder, faster and more furiously than the other, to the obvious enjoyment of all parties.

Ruben often played his melodian when on fogging duties in the daytime, but when he started to practise new tunes in the middle of the night, it caused the occupants of a row of cottages close to his signal to complain bitterly to Stationmaster Benjamin Harris, or "Snuffy 'Arris" as he was known to the staff, owing to the huge quantities of snuff he used to push up his nose.

"You know Owd Snuffy told you not to play that melodian in the night", the Signalman said.

"Ar thought it 'ud cheer em up a bit if they cuddna slape", Ruben remarked in all seriousness. "Wot about your mate in the next box", he suddenly enquired, "'im wot plays that owd 'ponium in the signalbox all night?" He was quite right

about that piece of information. The Signalman played the euphonium in a brass quartet and used to practise on his night shift.

When he first started to play the instrument some years before, there were many rumours in the village about the dreadful noises heard over the fields. Many tales were told to explain the noise. Escaped wild animals from a circus was one particular favourite. Parents kept in their children at night; some adults were frightened to walk home from the local tavern in the dark. It took a brave man to find the truth. The local poacher, with his living to earn, heard the noise one night whilst in the wood near to the signalbox. He traced it to its source and bravely climbing up a nearby signal post, he gazed in through the open window of the box and saw the Signalman with his steel-rimmed spectacles on the end of his nose, sitting under the oil lamp and blowing into a gret owd shiny tub thing wi lots o' pipes sticking out on it and mekhing "orrible noises", to quote the poacher's words.

As time went by, and with plenty of night practice, the Signalman mastered the instrument, formed a quartet and was in great demand at fetes and all festive occasions.

"There wasn't any houses near his box", the Signalman said.

"Nar, but it frit the life outer some folk

at fost. Nobody's frit o' me owd 'lodian", said Ruben. "But anyway", he concluded, "ar shannapley 'er afore its deelate." The Signalman could read music and played the church organ. He had tried many times to play a tune on Ruben's melodian, but he couldn't make anything of it at all. Ruben's gleeful comments every time he tried to play irritated him. "Yo canna wok 'er, Dad, yo canna wok 'er." So he stopped taking up the invitation when asked, "Yo 'ave another go."

The hand lamps were trimmed and lit. "Can we mash in your teapot?", the Signalman was asked. The kettle was boiling so bottles were soon filled with milkless tea and pushed into coat pockets. They also helped to keep the body warm.

Abe unwrapped a newspaper parcel. Inside were two thick slices of home cured bacon and half a loaf. "Cannajust warm 'er up a bit on your toasting fork me owd bod?" Abe asked, holding up a thick chunk of bacon. It was all fat except for a faint tinge of pink down one edge.

"You'll have to be quick then", the Signalman said, "it's time you were up at the signals."

"Ar, orrate", was the reply.

Abe stuck the two-pronged toasting fork, made with signal wire, into the bacon and held it in front of the glowing fire bars. It started to sizzle immediately, and drops of fat fell into the ash pan. He turned it round after a while, but soon the fat became soft and it dropped off the fork into the ash-pan. With a muttered curse, Abe speared it out, scraped off the ashes with his shutknife, and clapped it on his bread. He took a large bite and a long swig of tea from his bottle. The clock now said one thirty in the morning.

A surprised cry of alarm suddenly came from one of the fogmen.

"I anna got no stick nor coal up at me 'ut!"

"En you?"

"Norra lot", the others said in chorus. Out came the tea bottles to be left by the stove and picking up their hand lamps, they went out to the cabin. Soon great thumps and crashes were heard, and cries of, "'ode 'er 'ere", "Watch me foot!", "Shine 'er 'ere", "Ay up", "Watch that 'ommer, theyeds loose!" As one held the axe on a piece of sleeperwood, the other bashed the back of it with a keying hammer, in the yellow light of the lamps. After much effort, a pile of splintery sticks were assembled, three sack bags were found, the sticks shared out and carried back to the signalbox.

The Signalman was looking through the swirling fog from the doorway, "Are you about ready?" he asked anxiously.

"Ar", said someone, "con way aye a bitter coal?"

"Yes", said the Signalman, "be quick."

They picked all the best pieces of coal and filled their bags with as much as they could carry, then back up the stairs to the signalbox. They collected their tea bottles, food bags, boxes of detonators, flags and any old newspapers the Signalman could spare. Back down the stairs to pick up the sacks of coal and sticks. Ruben had his precious melodian in the flour bag hanging from a loop round his neck. Then, clutching their hand lamps, they staggered off into the foggy frosty night, looking as if they were all set to climb the north face of the Eiger.

Alone at last, the Signalman gazed round the box. The top of the cupboard was awash with paraffin; spots of it trailed over the polished linoleum mingling with the water that had dripped off their clothes. Bacon grease ran over the black leaded stove bottom. The white-scrubbed foot board at the bottom of the lever frame was covered with small black rings from oily boot studs; the black crescent outline of heel plates completed the pattern.

The kettle was empty. He vowed never to send for the fogmen again. But of course he would. He knew he would. The clock now said two o'clock in the morning.

Treacle Takes Charge

THE platelayers sat in the cabin looking out at the rain, it hadn't stopped all day. The Ganger, Owd Woody, Billy "Me legs wunna goo" Pottle and Treacle Belly so named after a generous girth held in with a length of discarded horse harness and a large brass buckle.

They had been playing dominoes all day, and now tired of that sat silent. The Ganger spoke, "Put some of that stick under the kettle and we'll have another mash." The fire had burned low, but the stick chopped from old pine sleepers still impregnated with highly flammable preservative quickly caught fire, crackling, spiting and throwing sparks up the chimney. They all watched the fire. The Ganger broke the silence, "Like a Felix rising from the ashes", he said.

He read a lot of papers and magazines and often quoted, or misquoted bits out of them to the others. He got them from the signalman, who got them from the porter, who rescued them from empty compartments on the trains.

"If a cat was sitting on them 'ot ashes eed soon be rising in the air", said Treacle with a laugh. "It wasn't a cat, it was a bird." The Ganger explained. "It was a Greek bird that was getting old and not feeling well so it sat in the ashes and got better. It's just a story."

The Ganger said. They all looked at him, and he wished that he had never mentioned the blasted bird. He once described the permanent way inspector as, "being like a sword of Dee Mackle Tees (Damocles) 'allus waiting to drop on us."

The rain had now stopped and he was saved from further questioning by the arrival of the junior porter known as "the Lad". "Eh up, Jimmy what are you up to?" they enquired, "The King is coming", he said excitedly, "He's coming for the shooting". Treacle cut him short, "Not 'im again, the last time we had to clean the track for miles." The Royal train often came along the branch line to stop at their station when the King wanted to spend a few days at the nearby Hall owned by Sir Joshua Crabtree-Bough.

The permanent way department were required to put a man on every bridge and cattle crossing until the Royal train had passed through.

"It's supposed to be a secret", the Lad said. "'Ow do you know then?" he was asked. "Because I was sweeping the Booking Hall out and I 'eard 'Owd Doggy' (Mr. Barker) the Station Master talking to your Inspector, Mr. Smallwood (known as 'Owd Sawdust') about it. He asked 'Owd Sawdust' if he could get his men smartened up a bit when the King came because some of them looked like a bundle of old rags", he said and

stopped, conscious of all eyes on him.

Treacle spoke first, "A bundl'er old rags?", he exclaimed his voice rising with indignation. "What do they mean?" They all looked at him, his corduroy trousers had all the cord worn off in large patches, his waistcoat was the recipient of a thousand spilt dinners with a slit halfway up the back to accommodate his girth, his jacket, holes in elbows, ragged at wrist, was fastened together with snare wire, topped off by his hat that looked like the very one worn by Guy Fawkes on the fatal night, but beneath that grimy exterior beat a heart of gold.

Treacle was a bachelor and his loves were beer, tobacco, food and his dog Fred. He walked the permanent way every day accompanied by Fred, knocking the wooden rail keys in and reporting any faults in rails or fences.

The railway ran through a large sporting estate which teemed with wildlife, pheasants, rabbits and partridge. Treacle and Fred knew them all and were familiar with their ways. Many an elderly person in the village found a "body" wrapped in a sack hanging in the outhouse plucked and dressed ready for the pot. His railway friends were always sure of a good dinner too.

One day when walking the length he found a dead barn owl. This was most unusual so he picked it up and put it in his "Diplomatic bag". A large bag he carried over his shoulder with spare rail keys inside. It was also the means of conveying fur and feathers away from the watchful eye of the gamekeeper.

At the cabin he took the owl out of his bag to show them. They were all interested, it was rare to see one at such close quarters, it brought forth comments like: "It's got a flat yed!" "So would you if you had been hit by a train!" "Its yed twists right round!" "It wunna peck much corn wi a beak like that!"

Treacle put the owl in his pocket (a large one cut in the lining of his jacket) and took it home. It was still there that night when he sat in the bar of his local tavern enjoying a pint of strong brew known as "Rat Killer", it was said the rats liked it and sometimes fell into the beer vats and were drowned.

He took the owl out of his pocket and studied it closely. "You're a funny owd bod", he said, "like a broad faced chicken." He started to laugh and asked the men in the bar, "Ever seen a broad faced chicken?" They all had a good laugh about it. The tale soon got round and for months after people would shout to Treacle, "Do you want to buy a broad faced chicken?", but he just grinned and took it in good part.

The Ganger had a letter from "Owd Sawdust", the permanent way inspector, outlining their duties for the Royal train and requesting they should be smartly dressed, promising no dirty tasks that day.

They all arrived at the cabin on the morning of the Royal visit in their Sunday clothes, they stared at Treacle in amazement. He had on a good pair of black trousers exchanged from the signalman for a pheasant, a black tailed coaching jacket with brass buttons that had belonged to his Uncle Bert, who had been a coachman at the Hall. A celluloid collar, black tie and bowler hat borrowed from his Cousin Joe who was a pall bearer in his spare time. A red rose in his buttonhole completed his satorial dress, plus a freshly shaved face.

He went up to the signalbox to the grinning signalman to borrow some Zebrite grate polish to smarten up his scuffed boots. Then they all went off to their allotted places on bridges and crossings. Treacle had to keep the sleepered crossing clear of people near to the end of the platform.

The pilot engine that precedes the Royal train went by and fifteen minutes later the monarch's train drew into the platform. Treacle lifted his bowler and smiled at faces looking out of windows, but it brought no response. They don't look very happy, he thought.

The Stationmaster all pressed and shining greeted the Royal visitors as they stepped off the train, escorted them through the booking hall to waiting vehicles and thence to the Hall.

The platform gradually cleared of people. Treacle, his duties finished on the crossing, strolled along the platform looking in the carriages.

A window was let down and a head appeared wearing a uniform cap that said "Guard". He spoke "Excuse me, sir." Treacle looked behind to see who he was speaking to, it was deserted, he looked back at the Guard who looked him straight in the eye, "Can you tell the staff where to unload the luggage please?" It suddenly dawned on Treacle he was being called SIR! He nodded, hardly being able to speak. Then followed the Guard through the train to the restaurant car and was asked to wait whilst staff were sought.

He gazed at the tables where the remains of a meal waited to be cleared. A door slid open at the end of the carriage and a white-coated figure appeared. "Hello", he said, Treacle felt he had to justify his position, "I'm waiting for the staff to come and unload the luggage so we can get the train away." "Have you had your lunch?" the white-coated figure asked. Treacle's brain went into top gear at the mention of food. "No", he said, "Me and my men have been guarding the bridges and crossings all day." "Come into the kitchen", he was told, "we've got plenty of food left."

A large dilapidated wicker hamper was produced and the white-coated man filled it with the remains of a cold luncheon, beef, pork, ham, chicken, pork pie, tomatoes, celery, pickled onions, a bag of cottage loaves and a large apple pie.

"Any beer?" asked Treacle hopefully, "No, they have drunk all the beer, the claret and the port." "Wot a lot 'er greedy guts", Treacle thought. "But" said White coat, "there's some red wine left they don't seem to like it, you can have those four bottles, it's full bodied, but a bit harsh on the palate." Treacle's eyes shone and his stomach revolved round at the sight of all the food and drink. "It's just what my men like", he said, "full bodied and 'er", he paused, "all that." "Have you any old bones for me guard dog? He has to guard, oooh, all sorts of things when the King comes, he's still at it now."

The truth was Fred was fast asleep on a bag in front of the fire in the platelayers' cabin. The only things he was guarding were the mice that played around him. He would have ignored them anyway, had he been awake, after chasing rabbits all day, Fred was not interested in mice.

The white-coated man went into the kitchen and came out with a bag of bones. Treacle thanked him and they fastened the hamper lid down.

The Guard came back with three staff

in tow, he pointed to Treacle. "This gentleman will show you where to put all the luggage." Treacle's chest swelled with pride putting extreme pressure on the buttons of his Uncle Bert's coaching jacket. To be called Sir or Gentleman all in one day was almost too much to take in, they would never believe him back in the cabin.

He soon had the staff unloading the luggage. Large chests, wicker baskets, hampers, suitcases, boxes, gun cases, boxes of cartridges, bundles of shooting and walking sticks and things bound up in hessian sacking. Treacle directed all operations. "Put that there." "Bring them over here." "Load that four-wheeled barrow." "Stack them trunks on top of each other, then take them round to the front of the station to await transport to the Hall."

The sweating staff obeyed all his commands. Treacle had never enjoyed himself so much. He was sorry when it was all unloaded.

His final command was to ask two of the staff to carry the wicker hamper with the food and wine in down to the platelayers' cabin, himself proudly walking in front.

When the staff had gone, Treacle opened the hamper with a flourish and spread the food out on some newspaper before his astonished companions.

Fred woke up, wagged his tail and got a bone. They all tucked in to the food, but the wine they said was sour, however a generous quantity of sugar added to the bottles and vigorously shaken, made it palatable, so it was all consumed.

It was certainly Treacle's day. All this free food and drink and to be called Sir and a gentleman was something to be relived and talked about for months and years to come.

"I 'ope 'ee comes again", said Treacle. But he never did.

The Shackerstone Mail

AS the nights draw in, and the oil lamps burn brighter in the museum at Shackerstone, it brings to mind the time when these lamps shone from the station and the posts all along the platform. A little old lady hurries along the dark station drive, holding the small mailbag, tied tightly at the neck and sealed with brown sealing wax, containing the outgoing Shackerstone Post Office letters. Some nights, there were only two, but they were just as important as a sackful. On a cold night, perhaps, there might be a short wait by the Porters' Room fire and a word with the Porter before the strident note of the platform bell let them know that the return of the five-ten Nuneaton-Ashby milk train was at hand.

A walk down the platform and over the sleepered crossing by the water crane to the upside as the train, a small tank engine and one passenger coach with a guards compartment, drew to a stop. The mail bag was handed to the Guard, and he in turn perhaps had a few railway letters and a parcel for the Porter before the doors shut with a crash. A touch on the whistle and the train was away, clink-clanking its way into the night back to Nuneaton.

One by one, the platform lamps went out and soon the station was in darkness, and the nightly ceremony of the Shackerstone mail was over; leaving only the glow from the signalbox and the lamp at the bottom of the steps to keep watch until morning.

Shackerstone, on the Ashby & Nuneaton Joint Railway.

Photographic Credits

* Shackerstone Museum Collection.

ASHBY, COALVILLE, SHACKERSTONE & NUNEATON LINE TO SHACKERSTONE :

LEAVE NUNEATON.	LEAVE HIGHAM-ON-THE-HILL.	LEAVE STOKE GOLDING.	LEAVE SHENTON.	LEAVE MARKET BOSWORTH.	LEAVE SHACKERSTONE.	LEAVE COALVILLE.	ARRIVE LOUGHBORO
a.m.							
7-22	7-31	7-36	7-41	7-47	7-57	8-17	8-42
9- 5	8-11	9-16 .	9-23	9-29	9-48	To Ashby	
—	—	—	—	—	10- 0	10-16	10-45
p.m.							
—	—	—	—	—	12-13	12-29	12-57
1-20	1-30	1-34	1-40	1-47	1-57	To Ashby	
—	—	—	—	—	2- 5	2-21	2-50
3-15	3-21	3-25	3-33	3-41	3-51	4-15	4-40
—	—	—	—	4-20SX	4-30	4-47	5-15
6-53	7- 0	7- 5	7-11	7-17	7-23	To Ashby	
7-30	—	—	—	7-42	7-51	To Burton	
—	—	—	—	—	8- 5	8-21	8-50
*8-27	8-33	8-38	8-44	8-49	8-55	To Ashby	
10-30SO	10-37SO	10-41SO	10-46SO	10-52SO	10-58SO	To Ashby	

* Midland Station.